THE CONTRACT FROM HELL

CONTAMINATED FAMILY HOUSING

NUCH RETLAW

The opinions expressed in this manuscript are solely the opinions of the author and do not represent the opinions or thoughts of the publisher. The author has represented and warranted full ownership and/or legal right to publish all the materials in this book.

The Contract from Hell
Contaminated Family Housing
All Rights Reserved.
Copyright © 2014 Nuch Retlaw
v3.0

Cover Photo © 2014 thinkstockphotos.com. All rights reserved - used with permission.

This book may not be reproduced, transmitted, or stored in whole or in part by any means, including graphic, electronic, or mechanical without the express written consent of the publisher except in the case of brief quotations embodied in critical articles and reviews.

Outskirts Press, Inc.
http://www.outskirtspress.com

ISBN: 978-1-4787-4069-8

Outskirts Press and the "OP" logo are trademarks belonging to Outskirts Press, Inc.

PRINTED IN THE UNITED STATES OF AMERICA

DEDICATION

This book is dedicated to Terry Metcalf and we must learn from his example to fight for righteousness. We dedicate this book also to the awareness of the military families living on contaminated lands. We are hopeful that our lawmakers recognize the horror that was created. It is our hope that the lessons learned from this story will inform military families of the hazards in and around their residences.

We are hopeful that our lawmakers will realize that the creation of laws and regulations must be enforced and must always consider the impact of such laws and regulations. Accountability is the element of effectiveness in our laws and regulations. It is the key principle of the public's trust that allows the assumption of good faith for all officials. Officials who violate laws and regulations violate the sacred trust given to them from the public and we cannot tolerate these violations.

ABOUT THE AUTHOR

The author was an active participant during the execution of this contract with the HUBZone contractor and the Department of the Navy. He provided consulting services both as the General Manager for the company for some of the time and as the Safety/Risk Manager at other times.

Often in the position of a "3rd set of eyes" he was able to advise the contractor regarding the execution of the contract. The seriousness of the issues presented by the Navy throughout the contract period was varied and frequent. These issues ranged from fraud, waste and abuse of authority, to identification of minor safety or workmanship issues.

These issues were often "blown up" and threats were made to stop the project or to relieve the project manager, superintendent, Quality Control manager or the site safety and health officer. The issues became a full time effort for the Project Manager who spent the majority of his time answering emails, investigating unsupported allegations, answering questions regarding the details of the project. The author assisted as the Project Manager when needed and corresponded with the Navy.

The author started this project from the onset when the project proposal was reviewed and the decision made to submit a proposal. The author participated in the discussions regarding the decisions to protest the initial award of the contract to a large business. And the author was the last person on the jobsite when the project completed.

The author actively participated in the development of the claim submitted and testified in the trial before the Court of Federal Claims. He assisted with the review of depositions and discovery data.

The author is an experienced safety and health professional with over 45 years of experience in the field of safety and health. He is experienced with safe exposure, identification and controls of chemicals and biological materials. Exposures to hazardous substances include work with radioactive materials, asbestos, and numerous chemicals associated with ship repair, the construction industry, the healthcare industry and general industry exposures.

This book represents the opinions and observations of someone who was present from the start to the end. The facts and the supporting information for these opinions and observations were personal and relied on the documentation produced during the discovery phases of the claim as well as the documentation collected during the execution of the contract.

The Contract From Hell—A HUBZone Business Story

Table of Contents

Introduction i

Chapter 1: Hubzone Preference 1

Chapter 2: Different Goals 7

Chapter 3: The Project Schedule: A Means to an End 17

Chapter 4: One Sided Qualifications 26

Chapter 5: Government Delays the Project 38

Chapter 6: Restrict Cash Flow 46

Chapter 7: Navy Contaminates the Housing Project 56

Chapter 8: Contaminated Housing Project Is Not Safe 61

Chapter 9: Cost of Contaminating a Housing Project 80

Chapter 10: Violation of Laws 88

Chapter 11: The Hubzone Contractor Is Alone 99

Chapter 12: The Contract from Hell 107

Chapter 13: Sins of the Navy 112

Chapter 14: Court of Federal Claims Decision 121

Chapter 15: Appellate Court Decision 130

Introduction

Small business is the pride of America and it allows us to be creative, innovative and self-reliant. The State of Hawaii's employers consist of about 97% Small Businesses as shown in the 2006 business demographics. The 2006 statistics also show that 97.5% of the businesses in the United States belong to small business. Congress recognized the strength of our small businesses and created the Small Business Administration (SBA) in 1953. Their purpose is to aid, counsel, assist and protect the interests of small business concerns, to preserve free competitive enterprise and to maintain and strengthen the overall economy of our nation. The SBA administers the small disadvantaged business programs for small businesses contracting with the Federal Government. These SBA programs establish "preferences" for award of contracts; to assist small businesses in working with the Government and promote use of small business.

One of these small disadvantaged business programs is the historically under-utilized business zones or HUBZone certifications. A small business operating in a HUBZone can be certified by the SBA and given a 10% preference in the competition for award of contracts with the federal government. The HUBZone Empowerment Contracting Program is an initiative by the SBA since 1997. The HUBZone is a preference for fair competition of contracts by a small business when competing against a large business.

THE CONTRACT FROM HELL

This is a story of a small disadvantaged business that fought the good fight for righteousness and accountability. There have been many horror stories of fraud, waste, and abuse of authority by government agencies for some time. These stories must be told and hopefully the lawmakers and responsible authorities will get the message that no one is watching the store and no one is held accountable for fraud, waste and abuse of authority. The most critical message is a notification to military family members on the Kaneohe Military Base Housing that they are living in homes constructed on lands contaminated with carcinogens.

There are many federal laws and regulations that are violated by the Navy. The effort to save money and to destroy the HUBZone business resulted in the contamination of a housing project that will produce a disproportionate risk of cancer to the unborn, the infants and children, and the pollution of the federally protected waters surrounding the marine base. The impact of these actions will continue for years and affect generations to come.

There is no excuse or reasonable rationale for completing this project and the end result is military housing on contaminated lands. The carcinogen contaminated housing project for our military is an atrocity of this project. The story does not end here because the prolonged exposure of the carcinogens to the infants, children and military families will continue for future generations. The contamination of our environment which includes the contamination of federally protected waters will continue for future generations.

1

Hubzone Preference

This is a story of a small disadvantaged business owner and the opportunity to improve by growing and developing long term goals to ensure jobs are created and sustained in the area of his residence, a historically under-utilized business (HUBZone) area. The HUBZone preference was created and approved by Congress for this purpose.

The Small Business Administration (SBA) implemented a program for the historically under-utilized business zones (HUBZones). This program gave small disadvantaged businesses who qualified for the HUBZone program to be given a preference in federal contracting. It also established a goal for federal agencies:

> *"The Government wide goal for participation by qualified HUBZone small business concerns shall be established at not less than 1 percent of the total value of all prime contract awards for fiscal year 1999, not less than 1.5 percent of the total value of all prime contract awards for fiscal year 2000, not less than 2 percent of the total value of all prime contract awards for fiscal year 2001, not less than 2.5 percent of the total value of all prime contract awards for fiscal year 2002, and not less than 3 percent of the total value of all prime contract awards for fiscal year 2003 and each fiscal year thereafter."*

THE CONTRACT FROM HELL

A small disadvantaged business must qualify through a certification process by the SBA to be eligible for competing in federal contracts. The preference for these businesses is a 10% preference awarded in their bid. For example, if their bid is $1,000,000.00; the next bidder, non-HUBZone business, is $980,000.00 and the third bidder, also a non-HUBZone business, is $975,000.00, the HUBZone business could be awarded the contract even though they were higher. The 10% preference is applied to each non-HUBZone bidder, thus the $980,000.00 bidder would be $980,000.00 + $98,000.00 = $1,078,000.00. The HUBZone business must also meet the requirements for technical evaluation, quality, management, experience based on past performance, etc. The price evaluation is the only advantage that the HUBZone business is given to help level the playing field when competing with qualified large businesses.

The intent of the HUBZone Empowerment Contracting Program is to improve the economic status of distressed communities. The federal contracts would be encouraging growth and long term development of businesses thereby creating jobs and attracting private investment. The goals in 2001 for "all U.S. government agencies" to award 2 percent of federal contracts to HUBZone businesses in 2001, 2.5 percent in 2002, and 3 percent in each year after were not met. We know that the federal agencies were slow in accepting the HUBZone program and their progress was poor. In 2000 the federal agencies reported that only 0.33 percent of their contracts were awarded to HUBZone businesses. The government was slow in accepting their responsibilities required by this new law. The Navy contracting office in Hawaii had not awarded <u>any</u> contracts to HUBZone businesses at the time of this story.

The Congressional intent to improve the economic status of distressed communities is ignored and the destruction of a long standing business in a distressed community is the result of the government officials' abuse of authority. The destruction of a small business does not speak well for the HUBZone program or the behavior of the government officials. We must look into the history of federal contracting in the area where this story occurs, the State of Hawaii.

HUBZONE PREFERENCE

The biggest island in the Hawaiian island chain is the island of Hawaii, often referred to as the "Big Island". This island is designated a HUBZone by the U.S. Census and therefore businesses that reside on the Big Island and who meet the qualifications are certified as HUBZone businesses by the SBA. Once certified and accepted in the program they are eligible to bid on federal contracts and could expect to be given the preference allowed by the HUBZone Empowerment Contracting Program established by the 1997 Small Business Reauthorization Act.

One of these small disadvantaged businesses is a general contractor with 25 years of experience, primarily in the residential housing field, who applied for the HUBZone. He met all of the requirements of the HUBZone Empowerment Contracting Program and was certified by the Small Business Administration (SBA). In 2001 he bid on a $48,000,000.00 residential design-build project for the U.S. Marine Base in Hawaii. He bid against two other large businesses for the same project.

Historically, the Department of Defense (DoD) in Hawaii was experienced in evaluating residential construction bids by the same three or four large businesses. In the previous 25 years these same companies were awarded all of the residential housing projects by the DoD in Hawaii. It was a nice arrangement because the government and the competitors were familiar with their request for proposals and bid proposals, as well as a close familiarity with each other. So familiar that the federal government contracting personnel were comfortable enough to call one of the large business bidders to illegally let them know there was an error in their bid so it could be corrected **prior to** award.

The 2001 bid was submitted by the HUBZone business and the Navy contracting office decided to "disqualify" the HUBZone business without informing them. A large business was awarded the contract. The HUBZone contractor decided to request a debriefing for the purpose of "lessons learned" for future proposals. During the debriefing he is informed that his bid was thrown out because he exceeded an ambiguous budget ceiling in one of the phases of the project, although the total bid was within budget. Confused and disappointed with the ambiguities they requested a review of the file. The HUBZone contractor was shocked to learn that the same error was committed by one of the large business competitors and that the government contracting personnel called them to correct the proposal <u>prior</u> to the award!

The federal contracting rules allow for any business to file a protest of the award if they believe something is not right. On the other hand a small disadvantaged business must consider a number of impacts to their company and their future before proceeding with such actions.

- The protest will delay the project and the bid bond for ~$48,000,000.00 will be held until the protest has been adjudicated. This means the HUBZone contractor is tying up a large portion of his bonding capacity and his ability to obtain other work.

- The legal costs are significant.

- The HUBZone contractor is not familiar with the process for protest. The rumor and gossip from others in the community is that "you can't fight City Hall".

- Would there be retribution, by the Navy, in future bids and projects?

This HUBZone contractor decided to proceed with the protest. There must be an understanding of the company and their beliefs to understand why they proceeded. The owner of this HUBZone business is an individual with a strong sense of patriotism, loyalty, dedication, and commitment. These characteristics are his strength and it is the motivation for his actions. At the end of the day his profit is a benefit not a motivator. He has 25 years of experience as a general contractor and has built numerous residential projects ranging from affordable housing units to custom high end luxury condominiums and townhouses. He was the primary contractor on the Big Island for the luxury time shares units that were being built during this time frame. He is definitely a qualified contractor and a patriot.

On September 11, 2001 the United States was attacked. The war had started and this patriot wanted to participate by supporting the troops. He would do what he does best, build houses for our military. This was a prime motivation for the bid proposal to construct 212 residential units at Kaneohe Marine Base in Hawaii. This company was doing well in the private sector and there was no need to get in to the federal contracting arena. The $48,000,000.00 project meant that he would be able to contribute to the quality of life for our soldiers. This one factor drove many of his decisions to protest the award and to be a participant in our country's efforts. He was told by many that he could not fight City Hall and expect to win or that there would be untold retributions to him and his company for fighting the government. His loyalty and his faith in our country drove him to believe that right will prevail.

This HUBZone contractor will show us that being a U.S. Citizen includes loyalty to our government. He believed firmly in the simple fact that the United States is right and that righteousness will always prevail. He stood by his belief that he did nothing wrong and that he was participating in the legal HUBZone program developed by Congress. Till this day his loyalty to his country, his family, workers and his company remains the strength in his survival. His loyalty has been viewed by many as foolish, but none the less it is characteristic of the U.S. Citizen and a small business owner.

The strength of loyalty must be accompanied by a dedication. His dedication to his goals and the participation in the effort to increase the quality of life for our soldiers became a major part of his life. He dedicated his efforts to this goal, his dedication to his workers and all of the people that worked on this project are strengths that were clearly recognized by all. It makes him a leader in his community and it is a shining example of his faith in others and his faith in our Creator.

The HUBZone contractor decided to protest the award to the large business as allowed by law. It was obvious that the Navy contracting personnel notified the large business of the same error as the plaintiff without notifying the plaintiff. The bias created by favoring one side over the other was considered inappropriate. The federal court ruled that the actions of the Navy contracting office was arbitrary and not in accordance with laws/regulations. The federal court ruled that the contract award to the large business be withdrawn and that the request for proposal be repeated. Award should be in accordance with law/regulations.

This is the starting point for the destruction of the HUBZone contractor. The sequence of events and the facts of the inequities and abuse of authority to fight the HUBZone laws by taking it out on a small disadvantaged HUBZone business are astounding. The lack of accountability and the blatant arrogance and incompetence of government officials to destroy a small business is a shocking reality of Federal Contracting. The Commanding Officer has a **duty** and a responsibility to ensure the laws are followed and that the abuse and the criminal activities eliminated, but in this case we see that the Commanding Officer of the Navy contracting office is at the front of this destruction. This decision by the federal court will be the first of three federal judges that decided that the Navy acted arbitrarily and not in accordance with law/regulations.

2

Different Goals

This is the story of a military construction project for multi-family residential units for the military families. The intent of Congress when it funded the military construction project was to improve the quality of life for our military and their families. The project consisted of 212 residential units constructed in duplex type buildings. These new buildings replaced older residential units that were about 50 years old. This project was a welcomed asset for the marines and their families at the Kaneohe Marine Base in Hawaii.

The intent of this project is lost in the execution of the contract. The Navy and the HUBZone contractor execute this contract with different goals. Because these goals were so vastly different this project becomes a disaster that is not consistent with the Congressional intent. The construction of high quality residential units was met with the cost being the destruction of the HUBZone contractor business and the unsafe residential areas to the military families. The intentional contamination of the front and back yards with known carcinogens directed by the government does not meet the criteria to improve the quality of life for anyone and flagrantly reflect the disregard for the intent by Congress. The Navy's goal becomes an attack to destroy the HUBZone business with the construction of the housing a secondary effort.

THE CONTRACT FROM HELL

The design build project was issued in early 2001 for 212 residential units with a budget of $48,000,000.00. A project of this size is considerable for a small business and certainly in the cross hairs of the large businesses. A small disadvantaged business with a HUBZone certification would have to ensure that the business assets were significant; that the performance and payment bond was available; and that the project staff and subcontractors were qualified and capable of a project of this size. There were three bidders on this project, two large businesses and one small disadvantaged business with a HUBZone certification. In September 2001 the government awarded the contract to a large business after unfairly disqualifying the HUBZone contractor.

The HUBZone contractor decided to request a debriefing to find out how it could improve their future bid proposals. At the debriefing they learned that they were disqualified because their bid exceeded the ambiguous budget by <0.01%. It was later learned that disqualification for exceeding the budget was based on the improper interpretations of the ambiguities in the proposal and disparate treatment of the HUBZone bidder.

The HUBZone contractor decided to file a protest and requested a decision by the United States Court of Federal Claims. The protest would take at least one year and during that period a $48,000,000.00 payment and performance bond was held in abeyance preventing the company from pursuing other projects. The decision to fight the ambiguities in the proposal, unfair treatment by the government evaluators, and arbitrary actions in the technical evaluation rankings was made with reluctance but in the interest of fairness and for the benefit of other small businesses as well. The court rulings:

"*CONCLUSION*
The court finds on each of the six counts as follows:

> *(I) Section 1A.7 is patently ambiguous rendering the solicitation defective. Plaintiff's duty to inquire was negated by defendant's duty, on this record, to notify, the failure of which prejudiced the*

DIFFERENT GOALS

plaintiff. **The Navy, thereby, failed to act in accordance with law/regulation.**

(II) The bidders were treated **unequally, thus unfairly,** *when one bidder received unequivocal clarification regarding the "budget ceilings" and the other bidders did not, constituting arbitrariness and acts by defendant not in accordance with law/regulation.*

(III) Although the Navy improperly evaluated plaintiff's overall rating for Factor C: Small Business Utilization due to its "NR" rating in subfactor 1, the result was harmless error.

(IV) The **Navy acted arbitrarily** *when it ranked plaintiff third technically, as said ranking is not supported in the record.*

(V) The **Navy acted arbitrarily, and otherwise not in accordance with law/regulation,** *when it eliminated [HUBZone Contractor] for exceeding a line-item budget ceiling, but did not eliminate another bidder who had previously committed the identical error.*

(VI) The Navy properly applied the 10% HUBZone preference for price evaluations, in accordance with law.

The Judge found that the Navy acted **unfairly, arbitrarily, and not in accordance with law/regulation** when dealing with the small disadvantaged HUBZone contractor for this project. The Judge's findings of unfair, arbitrary and not in accordance with law/regulation will repeat itself throughout the administration of this contract.

Historically, the Navy in Hawaii used large businesses to construct military family housing for 25 years. The long standing relationship with a few large businesses for this type of contract was upset with the introduction of the small disadvantaged HUBZone contractor. There are two significant impacts for this decision (1) the long history and practice of dealing with the same large businesses for housing construction contracts were now upset; (2) the Navy financial system for these projects has changed drastically because of the 10% preference. Assuming that the maximum budget for the construction project was $48,000,000.00 and the award to the HUBZone is at the maximum budget there would be no room for changes or upgrades. If the HUBZone business were not in the proposals the large business bids of less than $48,000,000.00 would allow an offset of monies to be used for changes and upgrades. The HUBZone 10% preference is a thorn in the Navy's side and the large businesses are caught off guard with the "new law" that had been in existence since 1997. How long did the government or large business think they had before this law would be implemented?

The interesting and notable observation in the cost proposals and the submission of bids by experienced large businesses with the federal government is that there is an unwritten "fudge factor" for change orders and upgrades. The HUBZone contractor was not familiar with the age old brotherhood that existed. A bid proposal based on the actual budget shown in the request for proposal is fair and the expectation by the HUBZone contractor is that this is a good budget figure calculated by the Navy; however this is NOT the reality.

The government and the large business operate in the "fudge factor" arena where their bids are substantially lower than the request for proposal affording the government use of the excess monies to address inadequate and incompetent requests to Congress for funding as well as deficient request for proposals. This is further discussed in subsequent chapters. Suffice it to say for now that the HUBZone contractor is not part of the brotherhood and does not know about or understand the "fudge factor game" and how to play. The Navy has to live with the deficient request for proposal and will have to deal with the inaccuracies and inefficiencies later and they are not happy.

The idea of a small disadvantaged business with a HUBZone certification with the financial backing, qualifications and experience to build a 212 residential housing project is a shock and a brand new

DIFFERENT GOALS

concept to both the Navy and the large businesses! Since 2001 there have been many more HUBZone and other small disadvantaged businesses that have been creative and innovative so as to be able to compete in larger markets with their preferences. But in 2001 this was a new concept in Hawaii and the large businesses and the Navy was forced to comply with the rules of fair play and small business preferences. It should be noted that the Navy was NOT forced by the Judge to award the contract to the HUBZone contractor but to re-announce and select the contractor in fairness and in accordance with law/regulation.

In late 2002 the contract was awarded to the HUBZone contractor. The Navy's contracting office manager met with the President and General Manager of the company and congratulated them on the award. He further informs them that in 25 years the Navy Facilities Command (NAVFAC) at Pearl and in the Pacific had never lost a protest. This was the first one and he thought it was interesting enough that we should know about it. *In retrospect this was probably a warning.* The blatant string of fraud, waste and abuse of authority by the Navy that followed was not expected and it was destructive. At the end of the day it is certain that the Navy's quest at the onset was to ensure that this HUBZone and others would not want to consider entering the federal contracting for these types of projects. Further the message that contractors cannot protest and win because in the long run they will be destroyed. They wanted to teach the HUBZones a lesson that resulted in the destruction of a successful small business. This becomes the primary goal of the project which is in direct opposition of the HUBZone contractor's goal of completing the project to produce safe quality housing.

The above perception is supported by another event. In late 2003 another housing project for 55 residential units at the same Marine Base was NOT awarded because of the HUBZone. The Navy concerns are expressed in an email requesting that the HUBZone requirement be removed from future solicitations:

"We are concerned that the award of the 55 housing project could

> *be again jeopardized by Hub-Zone. During the first time around, many contractors did not bid because of Hub-Zone was allowed. These contractors felt that 10% advantage to the Hub-Zone contractor was too difficult to overcome as this 10% represented the non-Hub-Zone contractors' profits. Consequently we had very few contractors bidding and these contractors were not experienced in big housing projects. I believe that there is <u>only one Hub-Zone contractor</u> in Hawaii and therefore, I believe that there would be no competition between Hub-Zone contractors. It is possible that with the inclusion of Hub-Zone, the award of this contract could fail again because of lack of interested experienced bidders. We have already been told by one experienced contractor that they will not bid if Hub-Zone is included."*

The HUBZone certification is perceived as a major problem and addressing the one HUBZone contractor in Hawaii becomes an initiative. At this time the "… *one Hub-Zone contractor in Hawaii*", is the one that was just awarded the 212 residential housing project. By December 2003 the Navy is trying to get bidders for the 55 design-build housing project and they are pretty sure that the one HUBZone contractor will be too busy to submit a bid on this project.

> *"My feeling is that _____[a HUBZone contractor] is too busy to submit a proposal for this project."*

One has to wonder why they thought the HUBZone contractor was too busy to submit a proposal for this project? At this time the Navy was delaying the 212 housing project and making it difficult for the HUBZone contractor to proceed with demolition and construction of the new project. The general attitude by the Navy towards the small business disadvantage programs reflects a disdain for small disadvantaged businesses. It is interesting that "F__" referenced below is the Navy's Small Business Advocate. Their internal correspondence reflects this disdain:

DIFFERENT GOALS

"As F__ said the Small Business Programs are social welfare programs. In the future and since small business is required by contracting, we should factor in these costs at the start of the project including the 1391 and CWE so that Congress funds these additional small business program costs and we design to the new reduced cost threshold."

We cannot overlook a proud history of unsuccessful protests against the Navy. The HUBZone contractor is informed at the time of award that the Navy has not lost a protest in over 25 years and that this was the first one. At the time the HUBZone contractor was in a mode of moving forward and completing a 212 residential unit project for the military families. The potential warning was not taken as anything more than a comment or a point of interest.

The impact of the HUBZone program means that the project simply has to be developed and awarded in an efficient and cost effective manner. This project is a design-build project which means the contractor owns the liability for the project. There is no reason for the government to interfere with the execution of the contract. At the end of the day the project must be completed with 212 quality residential units for the military. However, the government is not use to this kind of efficiency. The old practice of being able to award the project at a lower price, e.g., $43,200,00.00 would leave the government with the remaining 10% or $4,800,000.00 for change orders, upgrades and allow payment of ambiguities and errors in the request for proposal. This is a long standing practice of shoddy or improperly prepared request for proposals, and paying for it later. The following example illustrates this practice:

- The project is developed and a request made to Congress for the funding. The project soil is not properly classified to save money, e.g., a handful of soil samples are taken and an antiquated soil classification methodology used to save money.

THE CONTRACT FROM HELL

- Congress authorizes the project and issues funding for $48,000,000.00.

- The Navy issues the request for proposal (RFP) to the contractors and it improperly states that the soils are non-expansive and that no special engineering is required. The contractors have nothing else to base their proposal other than the erroneous and incomplete soil classification that was issued with the RFP and submitted to Congress.

- The contractor asks during the pre-bid period what would happen if the soils are found to be expansive. The response is that a change order would be issued.

- The contractors issue their proposals based on the improper soil classification and the contract is awarded. A large business known to the government issues a bid for $43,200,000.00 or lower knowing that future change orders to address the inefficiencies and inaccuracies of the RFP will be forthcoming. The HUBZone contractor submits an honest bid for the project based on the information provided and rely on the accuracy and efficiency of the RFP as required by law.

- Upon arrival on the site the contractor discovers that the soil classification is improper and that special engineering and materials will be required to accommodate the expansive soils. A change order is requested.

- Under the old system the Navy could address the inefficiency and inaccuracies of the RFP by issuing a change order to the large business. With the HUBZone the Navy is unable to issue a change order due to lack of funds because the award used up the budget. The root cause being the inefficiency and inaccuracy of the request for proposal.

DIFFERENT GOALS

The HUBZone contractor assumes at the start of the project that the primary goal is to complete the project and provide 212 high quality residential units for the marine families at Kaneohe Marine Base. The basic expectation of good faith and fair dealings is rightfully assumed. There are no expectations that the Navy will act in an arbitrary or unfair manner. Unknown to the HUBZone contractor the Navy's primary goal is not the same. The destruction of the HUBZone contractor and sabotage of the project appear to be their goal. Upon reviewing their actions there can be no other reasonable conclusion that can be reached.

As the project proceeds the HUBZone contractor encounters continued dishonest and bad faith situations and are not able to obtain fairness with the contracting officials. The abuse of authority and the plan to destroy and sabotage is blatantly obvious. Some examples of their actions are listed below:

- Manipulations and interference with the project schedule to develop justifications for delays and impose cash flow restrictions.

- Restrictions and interference on the allowance of qualified individuals for personal gain and to restrict progress of the project by not allowing qualified individuals to be used by the HUBZone contractor.

- Imposing inexcusable delays to the project at the HUBZone contractor's cost.

- Restricting cash flows based on schedule issues which were caused by the governments' manipulations.

- Bribery to eliminate modifications to the contract and to reduce the cost of essential modifications to the contract.

- Overzealous inspections and re-inspections to create delay, restrict cash flow, and cause liquidated damages.

- Assignment of contracting officers and staff that are not experienced or qualified for the administration of a residential construction project of this size and complexity.

- Intentionally exposing the future residents and their children to known carcinogens.

- Exposing the infants and children to disproportionate risks of cancer.

- Contaminating and polluting the federally protected waters surrounding the marine base.

The list of fraud, waste and abuse of authority was so blatant that it is clear that the goals of the contract were different. The HUBZone contractor is trying to execute a legally awarded contract and to complete the goal of providing high quality safe homes for the military families. The Navy is hell-bent on destruction and sabotage of the project and there is no evidence that their goal of the project was to complete residential housing for military families. The HUBZone contractor is doing everything within his power to proceed with the project and to simultaneously work "with" the Navy. Although the project is completed and the HUBZone contractor is proud of the quality of the housing it is not a safe place to live. The Navy's direction to build on contaminated lands created the problem for the military families now and the future. The starting point for the destruction of the HUBZone business on the project is the schedule.

3

The Project Schedule: A Means to an End

Normal construction management requirements require the construction schedule to form the basis for the progress of the project and payments. As work is completed the government and the contractor updates the schedule and payments are made based on mutual agreement of progress. If there are delays the government and the contractor enter the information and dates in to the scheduling software in preparation for the time impact analysis. The time impact analysis is the mutually agreed unbiased data that identifies the impact of time delays. The schedule becomes the common ground for progress, time impacts of delays, payments, and completion of the project. The Navy's Construction Management Program manual, P-445 describes the construction schedules:

"3.6.5 Construction Schedules

> *Schedules are required on most construction contracts and task orders issued by NAVFAC.* ***Depending on the specification requirements, the schedule may be anything from a single sheet hand drawn bar chart to a computer-developed Critical***

Path Method (CPM) schedule with many activities and relationships. The Government is required to perform a review on the Contractor's schedule and accept a "practicable" schedule. Neglecting to review and accept the schedule may be viewed as acceptance of the schedule as submitted. The Government's review will concentrate on specified scheduling requirements/constraints and contractually assigned responsibilities."

The schedule in this story is a horrific manipulation rather than the common ground for progress and completion of the project. It starts with unqualified, untrained and inexperienced contracting staff who will manipulate the schedule. They control the accuracy, sequence, and the updating of the schedule and use it as a tool to wreak havoc with the HUBZone contractor. The same manipulated schedule is used in the defense of the claims against the government.

P-445 is the Navy's "Construction Quality Management Program" and provides intent and the goals for the project from the Navy's perspective. We later learn that the government contracting staff is not trained or qualified in accordance with this manual. They lack the guidance, training and experience to understand the above concept of the project schedule. The untrained government contracting staff proceeds with the management of the project by ignoring the necessity of "accepting a practicable" schedule but uses the schedule to mitigate documentation of the government delays, to deplete the float and to develop a basis to defend against claims.

Note: Float is the time in a schedule that is not accounted for in the schedule or extra time that can be allocated for unforeseen delays, e.g., bad weather. The float belongs to neither party but used for the mutual benefit of completing the project.

The start of the construction timeline is mid-2003 when the HUBZone contractor is ready to start the demolition and construction of the 212 residential units. The design of the residential units

THE PROJECT SCHEDULE: A MEANS TO AN END

is in the final stages and the construction schedule is submitted for final approval. The government already accepted the project schedule submitted at the time of the proposal and the acceptance of the design schedule. The government arbitrarily decides that the specification that they approved earlier for the type of software to be used for the project schedule is not satisfactory. Instead of Microsoft (MS) Project they decide that they want Primavera Suretrack software. The HUBZone contractor is not familiar with this software and it is unusual since the MS project schedules were submitted with the project proposal and accepted by the government. Earlier in the project the MS schedule was also used in the design phase of the project. ***The only benefit of the change in software is to delay the HUBZone contractor.***

We later find out that none of the government contracting staff assigned to this project is trained or qualified to use the Primavera Suretrack software. And they do not use the software throughout the project. This one fact alone has significant impact to the overall issue of completing the project. The delay and imposition of new requirements for the schedule is only beneficial to the government in causing a delay for the start of the construction/demolition. This is the first step to the cause of delay and the process to deplete the float. Delays will later be blamed on the HUBZone contractor.

One of many plight or fight decisions for the HUBZone contractor is whether or not he should fight the technicalities of the government's attempt to delay the project or is it better to purchase the new software and to train his staff on these new requirements? The government alleges that they cannot use the MS schedule since their computers are loaded with the Suretrack software and they must be able to analyze the schedule and time impacts with this software. In the interest of good relations and good faith, the HUBZone contractor decides to purchase the new software and train his staff. This decision results in a delay to the approval of the schedule and work cannot proceed until an approved schedule is obtained. The HUBZone contractor has no reason to believe the government is depleting the float. After the fact we can look back and see that there is no rationale behind the delay other than to deplete the float early in the construction project. We also found that the Navy was in the process of developing a case to terminate the contractor, before work has even started, and delay is grounds for termination.

It is later discovered that the government contracting staff for this project do NOT have any training or qualifications for the use of the Suretrack software. The project contracting staff under oath testifies that they are not trained or qualified to conduct analyses of the project schedule using the Suretrack software. During the depositions it is learned that none of the government contracting staff is trained or qualified in the Navy's own Construction Quality Management Program requirements, P-445.

Schedule manipulations: The manipulation of the schedule by the Navy to ensure that the project completion date is not affected at the beginning of the project means that the HUBZone contractor cannot make any claims for delays, at least not until the float has been depleted. In July 2003 the HUBZone contractor notifies the government of a differing site condition with the expansive soils. The Navy's strategy is to not approve the project schedule software to cause a contractor delay while the Navy investigates the differing site condition. This action delays the start of the project which eats up the float time.

The following example illustrates the delay: The government is notified of a differing site condition in July 2003 and it is not resolved until August 2004. The delay and the impact of these delays must be reflected in the project schedule. This delay will show up in any time impact analysis and will change the project completion date. However, the government will not allow a schedule update to reflect these delays and they threatened the contractor. The contractor will not get paid if the schedule shows a late completion date. It is a "catch 22" if the contractor complies with the contractual requirement to update the schedule the government will not pay them. The government's manipulation of the schedule is planned and intentional to deplete the float in the schedule and to ensure that the contractor will not be able to claim for delays by the government. These kinds of manipulations can be seen as

THE PROJECT SCHEDULE: A MEANS TO AN END

the project progresses. The HUBZone contractor is held hostage and must make these changes to the schedule or they hold payments.

During the course of this project from early 2002 to early 2007, almost 5 years, there were only 8 approved project schedules by the government. The contract requires that a project schedule update be completed at least each month. This would have meant almost 51 schedules if the 9 months of design work is excluded. According to the specifications, payments to the contractor can only be made when the project schedule has been updated and approved, how is it then that the contractor was issued 36 payments during this period and there were only 8 approved schedules for the project? Further the specification required monthly updates and meetings:

"Meeting to update the schedule and the submission of an error free, acceptable updated schedule to the Government is a condition precedent to the processing of the Contractor's pay request."

At these monthly meetings one of the other actions required by the contractor and the government is to record the changes to the schedule as a result of modifications to the contract. However, there were no monthly meetings after the baseline schedule was approved in late 2003. The contractor scheduled the meetings and the government officials did not attend them. Looking back it is obvious that there was no interest for an accurate schedule and none of the government contracting staff assigned to the project were capable of evaluating the schedule anyway.

There were 10 contract modifications for this contract that contained extension of time. The contract specification requires that a fragnet be submitted with the contract modification. The fragnet is an analysis for the change in the schedule caused by any change orders. Any changes to the project schedule as a result of a contract modification cannot be completed unless directed by the Contracting Officer. The Contracting Officer would not allow any of the contract modifications to be inserted into the schedule in accordance with the contract specifications. This drove the inaccurate schedule. We found out later that the Contracting Officer was not trained or experienced enough to use the project schedule and to issue the allowance to conform the schedule showing the impact of the change order.

The Navy knew the project schedule was not accurate and would never be accurate because there would never be a conformance to include changes to the contract schedule. This also means the Navy violated the contract requirements and their actions are unreasonable. For the record the contract modifications added up to 512 days added to the project. It is inconceivable that the impact of adding 512 days to the schedule is not considered in the schedule or in the performance of the work by the Navy. It is later discovered that this is part of a continued effort to impact the performance of the HUBZone contractor, i.e., by using the inaccurate schedule as a performance factor for unsatisfactory ratings and later a cure notice. We find that the internal correspondence in August 2004 showed that the government contracting staff was already trying to default the HUBZone contractor. An inaccurate schedule may be a basis for default.

The HUBZone contractor is manipulated and forced to perform the actions required by the Navy in order to get paid. The issuance and maintenance of a project schedule that consists of the content required by the Navy and **not** reflecting the reality of the work allows the continued manipulations of the schedule by the government. The contractor is not allowed to move the contract completion date regardless of any impacts. The decree to the HUBZone contractor is that they will not get paid if the contract completion date is late. If the HUBZone contractor does not comply with the coercion by the Navy he will not get paid and the project will stop.

An example of the blatant disregard for their administration of a fair contract is demonstrated by the use of the schedule and the contract modifications to their advantage. During the construction a fiber optic cable was discovered that was not in the existing utility plans. There was a significant delay caused by the government's inability to identify who owned the cable and what it would require to relocate the

THE PROJECT SCHEDULE: A MEANS TO AN END

cable. The HUBZone contractor completed a time impact analysis of the schedule and submitted the fragnet and time impact analysis to the government. Since the government did not have anyone on the project staff that could evaluate the time impact analysis or the fragnet, they ignored it. They reduced the time impact to match their perception of how things should be rather than the truth. The HUBZone contractor asked for the government's evaluation of the time impact analysis to negotiate the time impact as required by the contract specifications and was not provided the evaluation (because there was none). They issued a unilateral modification to the contract for the delay on the fiber optic cable which was significantly less than the findings in the time impact analysis. The government later "blackmailed" the HUBZone contractor by requiring them to sign a "bilateral" modification for additional days in exchange for release of the illegally held retention. The hand written minutes by the Resident Officer in Charge of Construction (ROICC) is without a doubt, coercion and blackmailing. It showed:

```
Agreed To
1) ROICC Release $1.25m, retain $500k
2) ~~send~~ ROICC ltr rescinding claim
3) ~~sign mod providing 75 calendar days (18 add'l)~~ for FO cable making mod Bilateral.
```

The government violated the contract by **never using the project schedule** and the capabilities of the Suretrack software to evaluate and analyze the impact of the delay caused by the fiber optic cable discovery or any other delays. They with-hold retention and blackmail the contractor with contractor's monies earned to get the bilateral modification signed. This illicit activity puts the HUBZone contractor under duress to sign the bilateral modification which includes the release of "full satisfaction and accord". This action meets the criteria for bad faith because the Navy's actions are unreasonable and aimed at abrogating their obligations.

In 2004 the government issues interim unsatisfactory performance ratings and threaten to terminate the contract. One of their key allegations is the schedule updates and the inaccuracy of the schedule. The HUBZone contractor cannot have accurate schedule updates when they are not allowed to show real delays and cannot input the impact of these delays. The end result is an inaccurate project schedule which the contractor does not control. The schedule is manipulated and controlled by the government and the contractor does not have a say in the outcome of the schedule.

Other significant actions by the government are in the defense of the claim filed by the HUBZone contractor in 2007. The government's defense basically involves several analyses by an expert on the schedules submitted by the HUBZone contractor to the government. The development of the schedule issues for this project is not logical or justifiable. The history of the schedule issues reflect an attempt by the government to control the schedule and the outcome for the HUBZone contractor to ensure that he and other HUBZone contractors learn that they cannot use the HUBZone certification for big contracts:

- Require the use of Suretrack software that the government does not know how to use and the HUBZone contractor must learn how to use. This delays the project.

- Require the HUBZone contractor to update the schedule monthly with insufficient data, i.e., no conformance to include the impact of any delays to the schedule.

- Not allow the HUBZone contractor to update the schedule with the impact of real delays and forcing the use of the float by requiring that the contract completion date cannot be late or payment will not be released.

THE PROJECT SCHEDULE: A MEANS TO AN END

- The government alleges that the schedule is not accurate and threatens termination of the contract.

- The government defends the claim against them by analyzing and using the schedules that they manipulated and controlled throughout the contract.

Does any contractor expect the owner or customer to manipulate the schedule to defend against claims at the onset of a project? Would any contractor expect unqualified contracting staff to manipulate the schedule? It is a reasonable assumption by the HUBZone contractor that the government contracting staff is qualified and experienced to administer this contract. It would be bad faith to sabotage this project by assigning unqualified and inexperienced management.

4

One Sided Qualifications

The request for proposal for the project requires experience and qualifications for the contractor's key personnel, i.e., project manager, project superintendent, and Quality Control (QC) manager. The requirements are:

"The Offeror's qualifications and experience of proposed key personnel (project manager, project superintendent, and QC manager) will be evaluated based upon projects within the last ten years involving the construction of multi-family dwelling units or similar type facilities (e.g. townhouses, cluster type housing development, zero-lot housing development and single-family housing units in multi-family housing developments) of similar scope/dollar value/complexity as the proposed project. Offeror's submission is limited to not more than 10 most recent active/completed projects of similar scope/dollar value/complexity for each key personnel within the last ten years."

The initial award of this project to a large business was protested and the Judge found that the actions of the Navy were arbitrary and unfair. The process for the protest was over one year and the key personnel in the original proposal had to be replaced. The contract allows

ONE SIDED QUALIFICATIONS

the substitution of key personnel as long as the Contracting Officer is notified and the new personnel meet "comparable" qualifications. The requirements for substitution of key personnel are:

> *"The Contractor shall provide complete resumes for proposed substitutes, and any additional information requested by the Contracting Officer. Proposed substitutes should have comparable qualifications to those of the persons being replaced. The Contracting Officer will notify the Contractor within 15 days after receipt of all required information of the consent on substitutes. No change in fixed unit prices may occur as a result of key personnel substitution."*

There were four project managers, five project superintendents, and the QC manager position changed at least nine times during the course of the construction of this project. Over a four year construction period the turnover of project management staff is by any measure of performance, high. The reason for the high turnover can be seen in the following overview:

\multicolumn{3}{c}{PROJECT MANAGER}		
No.	Reason	Govt Directed Action
1	Left the project during the startup of the construction due to family illness	No
2	Project Manager allowed to work on site, ~4 months, but later rejected by the government	**Yes**
3	Interim Project Manager for ~5 months. New Project Manager hired from the mainland for ~5 months.	**Yes**
4	Govt recommended that the Project Superintendent be the Project Manager, who finished the project.	**Yes**
\multicolumn{3}{c}{PROJECT SUPERINTENDENTS}		
1	Original Supt did not start the project due to the length of time for award.	No
2	Supt on site and approved by the government.	No

THE CONTRACT FROM HELL

3	Government recommends that the Project Superintendent assume the Project Manager position.	**Yes**
4	New Project Superintendent completes the construction of the buildings and resigns.	No
5	New Project Superintendent finishes the project.	No
	QC MANAGER	
1	Original QC Manager left before the project started.	No
2	QC Manager hired by the contractor starts the project and was rejected by the government after ~3 months.	**Yes**
3	QC Manager subcontracted as required by the government and resigns ~7 months after being hired as directed by the government. Note: The direction by the government to hire a subcontractor with personal ties to the government contracting official is a conflict of interest. This conflict is ignored by the government and it results in a $240,000.00 contract to the friend of the government official.	**Yes**
4	QC Manager submittals rejected by the government. The government directs promoting one of the inexperienced QC Specialists to the QC Manager position.	**Yes**
5	QC Manager resigns after poor performance.	No
6	The replacement is directed by the government. They direct hiring QC Manager number 4 again, who again resigns after ~3 months	**Yes**
7	The contractor hires another QC Manager from Kona, Hawaii who resigns after ~9 months	No
8	The contractor hires QC Manager number 2 to complete the project	No
9	The QC Manager resigns due to serious illness after ~12 months. The contractor moves the project engineer to the QC Manager position. This individual had been rejected by the government for the QC Manager position several times, although he was accepted as the alternate QC Manager for most of the project.	No

ONE SIDED QUALIFICATIONS

The change of staff due to the government ***directed*** actions in at least 44% of the time is, without a doubt, interference by the Navy. The HUBZone contractor was informed on many occasions that he was a HUBZone contractor and not experienced in "government contracting" and that it was a limitation on his abilities to perform. The staffing of this project is one of numerous interferences by the government. The HUBZone contractor is at the government's mercy and must accept their direction to use unqualified personnel or personnel in a "conflict of interest". We now know that the government contracting staff was unqualified, untrained and inexperienced to administer a contract of this size and complexity. Their efforts to prevent the HUBZone contractor from using highly qualified, trained, and experienced personnel is explained by their intimidation of such expertise.

The position of the Navy in regards to the HUBZone contractor is best explained in correspondence between the Senior Executives in the Navy. In an email between the NAVFAC Hawaii/Pacific, Rear Admiral, and the Marianas Senior Executive, Rear Admiral the position of the government is clearly stated:

> *"We are all over this one—amazing that he brought it up with you. This contractor has had a housing construction contract since Oct 02 and has yet to complete a single unit. He claimed a differing site condition at one point, but it has been disproven. He exhibited poor workmanship, <u>unskilled people in the leadership positions,</u> late submittals and reports, and unsafe practices. It was a **"forced"** HUBZONE award after protests and award issues. He is under a cure notice now."*

The most threatening and horrific reality is that the inappropriate dealings with the HUBZone contractor who was legally and fairly awarded a residential construction project was being directed by the highest level in the Navy Facilities Engineering Command (NAVFAC). The HUBZone contractor was awarded the contract because it was fair and in accordance with the law/regulation. At the time the HUBZone contractor had no way of knowing that the highest level of NAVFAC considered this a *forced contract*.

The government's perception that the HUBZone contractor is unskilled in the leadership positions is a direct result of not being able to manage and staff the project with his own people. The qualifications and capabilities of a HUBZone contractor to bid on a $48,000,000.00 residential project contain risks and liabilities. The contractor must have the qualifications and experience necessary to perform such work and they must demonstrate their qualifications to others supporting the company.

> First the contractor must prove to their bonding company that they possess the experience and qualifications to complete a project of this size. The acceptance by the bonding company alone is a significant factor in the determination of qualification and experience. This contractor had over 25 years of residential construction experience and had successfully built major residential construction projects. This contractor was building time share residential units that are far more complex and detailed than the military residential units. Custom residential units were retailing on the open market for over $1,000,000.00 per unit. There is no question that the contractor, given the ability to staff and manage this project, would have been able to complete the project with the highest level of quality, on time, within budget and safety. The government interference with the qualification and experience of the key personnel were part of the steps toward destruction of the HUBZone contractor.

> Second the HUBZone contractor was awarded this project based on the qualification factors provided by the government. In the award of the project the government evaluated the factors for award and concluded that the HUBZone contractor was qualified and experienced enough to perform the work of the project. ***No one "forced" the HUBZone on the government.***

ONE SIDED QUALIFICATIONS

Third the HUBZone contractor learned that the acceptance or non-acceptance of the key personnel by the government would be based on their desire to control and sabotage the project. The provisions in the contract are subjective and allow manipulations to affect the key personnel positions on the project. The enforceability provision in the contract allows the government to control any substitutions.

> *"1B.7 ENFORCEABILITY OF PROPOSAL. The proposal must set forth full, accurate and complete information as required by this solicitation. The Government will rely on such information in the award of a contract. By submission of the offer, the offeror agrees that all items proposed (e.g., key personnel, subcontractors, plan, etc.) will be utilized for the duration of the contract and any substitutions will require <u>prior Contracting Officer's approval</u>."*

The control of the key personnel is only the tip of the iceberg. There are significant events that demonstrate the blatant manipulation of the key personnel on this project. These manipulations result in the Rear Admiral's statement regarding the HUBZone contractor's *"...people in the leadership positions unskilled."* This may be true since 44% of the time the government dictated who the HUBZone contractor could use as key personnel! There are two events that provide an example of the Navy's control of the project management. These events involve the negotiation of the Project Manager position where the government offers to release retention if the HUBZone contractor replaces the highly qualified and experienced Project Manager; and the second event involves the government's insistence that they award a $240,000.00 quality control subcontract to a company that has a personal relationship with one of the government officials.

In February 2004 the project is in the process of demolition and construction of the concrete slabs for the buildings. A new project manager is located and he is highly qualified since he has worked on various residential housing projects of similar size and complexity; he is a reserve Naval Officer and a qualified assistant resident officer in charge (AROIC); he is also an instructor for the Navy to train resident officer in charge of construction classes; and he is a qualified "expert witness" for construction claims. His experience and qualifications in the federal contracting rules and regulations are significantly greater than <u>any</u> of the government contracting staff. His resume is submitted for approval and the government provides a tentative verbal approval. Upon his arrival he is met with resistance from the government as he proceeds with the management of the project and the attempt to resolve the on-going issues. The government's resentment about having a qualified Project Manager with this kind of experience is uncomfortable and they notify the HUBZone contractor of their unhappiness. The HUBZone contractor has no choice but to release the Project Manager in exchange for release of retention to allow the project to continue. The minutes and follow-up to this meeting states:

> *"This provides a written followup to our discussion this afternoon. In summary I have decided to replace the current Project Manager, N--- F-----, effective July 16, 2004. The General Manager, W----- C---, will assume the responsibilities of the Project Manager during the interim until a suitable Project Manager has been employed and approved by the ROICC. Per our discussion and mutual understanding, the interim replacement is satisfactory and will meet the requirements to immediately release the $100,000.00 retention and to bring M___ into compliance with the contract."*

It is later learned through the discovery process that **NONE** of the government's contracting personnel have any experience on a design-build residential construction project of this size and complexity. The initial qualifications of this HUBZone contractor by the government was correct, they are qualified and experienced to perform the work of this project. On the other hand the government contracting personnel were NOT trained, experienced or qualified to administer a project of

ONE SIDED QUALIFICATIONS

this size and complexity. The continued efforts and the continued rejection of applicants for the project manager position continued until the government recommends that the current Project Superintendent be promoted to the Project Manager position. The Project Superintendent is not qualified per the qualification requirements previously imposed by the government contracting personnel.

The second blatant and outright fraud and abuse of authority is demonstrated by the qualifications for the QC Manager. An accepted QC Manager must be on site before any work can proceed. The contract requirements for the qualifications of the QC Manager are:

"QUALIFICATIONS: An individual with a minimum of 5 years experience as a foreman, superintendent, inspector, QC Manager, project manager, or construction manager on similar size and type construction contracts which included the major trades that are part of this contract."

The HUBZone contractor decided to substitute the QC manager with another. The government continued to reject QC Managers with numerous years of experience and qualifications. The government insisted on the use of two individuals for QC Managers. A table of the types of qualifications that were accepted and rejected by the government is shown below:

QC Mgr	Supvy Experience	Yrs of Experience	Residential Experience	Bldg construction experience	Gov't (R= reject; G= Govt directed; C= contractor hire
1	Yes	35	Yes	Yes	R
2	Yes	32	Yes	Yes	Contractor terminated
3	Yes	19	Yes	Yes	R
4	**No**	22	No	Yes	G
5	No	17	<5 yrs	Yes	G

THE CONTRACT FROM HELL

The insistence that the HUBZone contractor use a subcontractor, see QC Manager No. 4 above, that does not meet the qualification requirements is questionable. This subcontractor receives a subcontract for ~$240,000.00 for providing the QC Manager and quality control testing for the project. It is later discovered that the government contracting person that rejected the qualified QC Managers in favor of the unqualified, inexperienced subcontractor had a past personal relationship with the subcontractor. The depositions also revealed that the government directed QC Manager was dishonest in his resume claiming that he had a college degree when he did not. Not only is this a conflict of interest but it is puzzling to the HUBZone contractor.

Perhaps the motivation was staring the HUBZone contractor in the face. During the periods that the unqualified and inexperienced government directed QC Managers were on the project we note that non-compliance notices were issued by the government. Non-compliance notices are notices issued by the government to notify the HUBZone contractor of non-compliant work and a request to initiate corrective actions. The following table clearly reflects the inexperience and lack of qualifications of the government directed QC Managers. The HUBZone contractor again is puzzled by this predicament and the motivation for such actions.

Alternate QC Manager and Time of Service and Non-Compliance Notices (NCN)			
Dates of Service	QC Manager	NCN	Comments
7/14 – 7/25/2003	Alternate		
09/20/2003 – 1/8/2004	**Gov't directed**		
1/9 – 1/23/2004	Alternate	1	The NCN was issued immediately after the Govt approved person left for vacation, although the work in question occurred during his watch.

ONE SIDED QUALIFICATIONS

Alternate QC Manager and Time of Service and Non-Compliance Notices (NCN)			
Dates of Service	**QC Manager**	**NCN**	**Comments**
1/24 – 3/4/2004	**Gov't directed**	2, 3	Both notices issued at Gov't directed QC Mgr request. The work occurred on his watch and he took no action to correct the situations.
3/8 – 4/16/2004	Alternate		
4/19 – 4/22/2004	Alternate		
4/22 – 4/26/2004	Contractor hire		
4/27 – 9/7/2004	**Gov't directed**	5, 6	Both NCNs occurred while the QC Mgr was present. He took no actions to correct and in both situations concurred that the work was proper.
9/8 – 10/1/2004	Alternate	7, 8, 9	NCNs issued because of disagreement with the interpretation and application of the specs which occurred during Govt **directed QC Mgr period of service.**
10/4 – 12/23/2004	**Gov't directed**	10, 11, 12	Safety issues where Govt directed QC Mgr refused to followup on safety performance although required by the QC Plan.
12/27/2004 – 1/2005	Alternate	13, 14, 15, 16, 17, 18, 19, 20, 21	Minor discrepancies most of which are in dispute. Five of them issued on 1/12/05 at the end of the business day to support their disapproval of the contractor's hire as the QC Mgr. **These NCNs occurred during the period of the Govt directed QC Mgr performance.**

The review of this table establishes that 16 of the 20 non-compliance notices were issued while under the purview of the government directed QC Managers. The issuance of 5 non-compliance notices occurring in one day and immediately following the resignation of the government directed QC Manager on December 23, 2004 is a blatant <u>abuse of authority</u>.

One other interesting and confusing factor is the qualification and experience of the government contracting staff on this project. It was discovered that the government contracting staff was not qualified, trained or experienced in the design-build contract administration, and none of them had administered or managed a project of this size and complexity. In other words none of the government contract personnel met any of the qualification requirements imposed on the HUBZone contractor for this contract. It is also interesting to note that during the depositions the government contracting personnel that were responsible for quality assurance on the project had not been trained on the requirements of their own quality control program, P-445, "NAVFAC Construction Quality Management Program".

In retrospect and in view of other extenuating circumstances the motivation for such blatant actions against the HUBZone contractor is obvious. The HUBZone contractor did not know or realize during the contract period that:

- The government viewed the award of their contract as being a "forced HUBZone" contract. The HUBZone contractor would rightfully assume that he would be treated fairly and in good faith once the contract was fairly awarded.

- The government controlled a key element of the performance of the contract by directing the key personnel of the project. Preventing the HUBZone contractor from hiring people with known experience and qualifications results in the control of the project management in the hands of the inexperienced and untrained government officials.

ONE SIDED QUALIFICATIONS

- The government contracting personnel did not have the qualifications, training or experience in the design-build contract area or of a project of this size and complexity.

- The government control of the schedule to delay the project and to deplete the float, to prevent accuracy of the schedule, and to use the inaccurate schedule against the HUBZone Contractor in performance ratings and defense of the future claim was intentional.

- The government's control of the contract can be used to control the later efforts to defend against a claim, e.g., the allegations of poor leadership is later used to profile the HUBZone contractor not only by the Rear Admiral for NAVFAC Hawaii but the attorneys' defense against the claim.

The HUBZone contractor had no expectations that the government would direct and exploit delays to restrict cash flow and to hinder the HUBZone contractor's performance. There is no acceptable or reasonable justification for the assignment of government contracting personnel who are not qualified or experienced on this project. Is this not a violation of the good faith and fair dealings covenant? The expectation of fair dealings and good faith is the norm for construction work. As we piece some of the unknowns together with the known facts we see a trend in the unfair treatment of the HUBZone contractor. The military construction project is funded by Congress and the intention to construct quality houses for our military is the goal. The HUBZone contractor provided qualified and experienced managerial staff who were disapproved or removed by the Navy's actions. The Navy Officials are not qualified, experienced or trained to administer a contract of this size and complexity and it is reflected in their delays and abuse of authority. The HUBZone contractor cannot see any possible benefit in delaying the project. We should discuss these delays and the impacts. Who and how did these delays benefit anyone? Are these delays justifiable or is it just part of the scheme for destruction of a HUBZone business?

5

Government Delays the Project

During the administration of the contract the HUBZone contractor must assume that there is good faith by the government contracting staff. What justification is acceptable for delaying the project and driving the cost of the project higher? We now know that the head of NAVFAC Hawaii/Pacific was **"forced"** to award this contract to the HUBZone contractor. The efforts to discredit and destroy the HUBZone contractor are lessons to others. There are no other justifiable reasons for the many delays by the government. There is no benefit whatsoever to the government or to the HUBZone contractor to delay the project. The only consequence of the delay is to move the contract completion date outward so that liquidated damages could be assessed to the HUBZone contractor.

The project starts with a series of start and stop events that is damaging to the HUBZone contractor and his subcontractors.

- Changing the scheduling software and delaying the approval of the baseline schedule to delay the start of the project. This eats up the float on the schedule and rapidly puts the HUBZone contractor at risk for liquidated damages.

- The Design team and HUBZone contractor informed the

GOVERNMENT DELAYS THE PROJECT

government in July 2003 of a differing site condition. This issue is not resolved until August 2004. There is no justifiable reason for not providing a response to the HUBZone contractor for over 1 year, other than to delay the start of the construction. The obvious justification is to delay the project and to deplete the float at the start of the project.

- The government stopped the HUBZone contractor from working when they decided to proceed with work at their own risk. The reason was a change in the paperwork. The government stops a $48,000,000.00 project and impacts the performance of the project to require written specifications to be moved from one document to another. A form over substance requirement that caused an unjustified delay.

- The government directs additional soil sampling in the middle of the project and pesticide contaminated soils are identified in July 2005. A resolution is not provided to the HUBZone contractor until December 2005. Contract specifications for the handling of chlordane contamination on the project site are already included in the contract. The HUBZone contractor is deliberately stopped and not allowed to proceed with handling the chlordane contaminated soils in accordance with the contract. The delay from July to December 2005 impacted the HUBZone contractor and their subcontractors. The end result is the use of contaminated soils on the project and significant delays to the HUBZone contractor. The impact of these delays to the subcontractor is not considered or allowed by the government. The final consequence is liquidated damages to the HUBZone contractor; a contaminated housing project for the military families; and the pollution of the federally protected waters surrounding the marine base. The only reason for this delay is the attempt to save money and to pass the costs to the HUBZone contractor.

- The government decides to treat the HUBZone contractor differently when it comes to the building turnover inspections. By overzealous inspections, delays in the conduct of the inspections, and compounding the landscaping issues the occupancy of the buildings are delayed. The government official declares "WAR" on the HUBZone contractor and delays the inspections. Again there is no benefit for these kinds of delays other than to extend the contract completion date to allow the assessment of over $3,500,000.00 in liquidated damages.

- During the course of this contract 29 contract modifications are issued with 10 of these modifications involving time extensions for a total of 521 days. As discussed in the previous chapter on scheduling, the impact of the delays to the HUBZone contractor are not evaluated so the "real" delays are not reflected in these modifications. The manipulations by the government throughout the contract period did not allow the production of an accurate schedule. An in depth analysis or any other analysis of the schedules cannot be performed because the schedules are not accurate. The government contracting staff ensured that there would not be a means to accurately determine the delays and the impact of these delays that they would alleged is the responsibility of the HUBZone contractor. This would allow the government to defend against any claims and would allow the assessment of over $3,500,000.00 in liquidated damages.

No motivation to complete the project. Throughout this project one of the observations is the lack of motivation to complete the project. From the position of the Rear Admiral at NAVFAC Hawaii/Pearl that this is a "forced HUBZone" project to the construction engineering technician who declares WAR on the HUBZone contractor, it is clear that the completion of this project is not a common goal. One of the most blatant and obvious examples of the delays is in the manner

GOVERNMENT DELAYS THE PROJECT

in which the project would be completed and the units turned over for occupancy. If the common goal of completion is shared then this phase of the project is the most exciting and the most cooperative. Final inspections and corrections of minor discrepancies to allow the turnover of the units for occupancy should be a simple process.

This HUBZone contractor has over 25 years of experience in building high end duplexes, and townhouses. The value of these units is in the $1,000,000.00 range and the customer's satisfaction a high priority. The inspections of completed units for these types of projects include inspectors from financial institutions, the developers, the owners, realty sales staff, and often include insurance representatives. It is not uncommon to have a large entourage during these turnover inspections. However on this project the government inspectors and the housing representatives provide the inspection team for the turnover inspection. The conduct and behavior of the government inspectors required initial inspections, and second and third and sometimes fourth inspections prior to the turnover. Each inspection would identify new items so that the inspection process became a never ending process of minor issues and delays.

The overzealous inspection techniques involved absurd and ridiculous actions that clearly revealed the efforts to delay the project and the turnover of the buildings. A few examples of these actions are:

- Inspecting the living room wall by standing less than 12" from the face and observing the wall one square inch at a time.

- Identifying over 25 discrepancies on a front door with colored tape. These included nicks, or spots, or faded areas.

- Using a mirror to inspect areas behind doors, or top of doors, or behind appliances.

- Identifying a pin hole below a shelf in the pantry.

THE CONTRACT FROM HELL

- Crawling on the floor with 12"x12" linoleum floor tile to identify "volcanoes".

- Standing in front of a closet and opening and closing the doors in excess of 25 times.

- Inspecting screws on the hinges of the cabinets, and closet doors.

- Operating the light switch in a bathroom over 25 times.

The coordination of the government inspectors and the process for completing the punchlists becomes a battle with the government. There is no better way of explaining the situation other than the government inspector's own statement. The inspector declares "WAR" on the HUBZone contractor after citing a 1/64" discrepancy on a countertop. The government inspector testifies in his deposition:

"Q Do you recall having a conversation with M----- F-------- during which you said something along the lines of, quote, I like you guys and if it was just you, I would let things like this pass, but, unfortunately, this is a war and f---- J_____ O------ and G_____ A----

A Yes"

The end users of the project are the Marine Housing department responsible for placing the occupants in the units. One of the participants of the inspection party is the Housing department representing the end users although they have no authority to direct the contractor. Their participation is normally to observe the turnover process. One of the housing representatives relates his dissatisfaction with the building turnover inspection process in an email he issued to his superiors:

GOVERNMENT DELAYS THE PROJECT

"I have seen paperwork and heard talk of home acceptance inspections running two and three FINALS after the initial acceptance inspection and follow-up. These additional inspections have new items notes to the units are held from turnover to Housing Office. This does not seem right legally, correct me if I am wrong please. Also some of the items I am seeing that are made and issue of are trivial at best and on previous sites these have been rolled over into Warranty issues with out blinking an eye (i.e., Hunt's 237 Hawaii Loa, Fletcher-Pacific's 54 and Hunts 184) in order to give our customer, the service member, the ability to move in to the homes. That we are under duress to move our service members out of PPV area's we should take active roll in this process to have the homes passed over in a timely manor[sp]."

Note: Hunt and Fletcher-Pacific mentioned above are large businesses.

WHY? The most pertinent question with regard to government delays is why did the government cause these delays? Why would the government delay a $48,000,000.00 residential housing project when the need for family housing for the military families is a high priority? The government requires liquidated damages of $291.00 for each unit per day. This could mean it costs the government that much money while the project is delayed. To put this in perspective consider that 212 residential units are delayed for one month which equates to a cost to the taxpayers or the HUBZone contractor of $183,330.00 per month! Delays are costly to both sides.

The trend in the governments' actions or reaction to problems that occurred on the site was to <u>delay the response</u> to the HUBZone contractor. The response on the expansive soils took over 1 year; the response to the hauling of excess soils and debris took 2 years and the response regarding the chlordane contamination took ~5 months. The Federal Acquisition Regulations require the contracting office to investigate the site conditions promptly after receiving the notice of a differing site condition. It is not unreasonable for the HUBZone contractor to expect a prompt response from the governments' contracting staff.

The discovery process provides some of the rationale for the delays. In the differing site condition regarding the classification of the soils the government contracting staff hedge back and forth with no real decisions being made. They attempt to legalize their position that it is not a differing site condition rather than pursue the technical determination regarding the soil that is needed. This delay for over 1 year ends with a determination that they disagree with the test methods that were used. It should not take over 1 year to decide that they disagree with the test methods. They did not determine if the expansive soil would be a detriment to the construction of the housing units. The only benefit was to delay the construction project and to deplete the float in the schedule.

The delay caused by the chlordane contamination is inexcusable and an absolute atrocity. The government specifications for handling chlordane were already in existence and part of this contract. The governments' direction to NOT follow the contract documents resulted in a delay. The government specifications would have required the contaminated soils to be removed from the site and the site covered with clean topsoil. The governments' action to intentionally spread the contaminated topsoil and expose the residents to an increased risk of cancer is an atrocity.

We later discover that none of the government contracting staff are qualified, trained or experienced in the administration of a design-build project of this size and complexity. Their inexperience and lack of knowledge is demonstrated by their inability to deal with the issues of the differing site conditions as they arose. The government does not address the delays caused by the chlordane contamination and the impact of these delays. The time impact analyses submitted by the HUBZone contractor are ignored and the inexperienced and unqualified government contracting personnel cannot evaluate the schedule impacts.

A cause and effect analysis chart illustrates and summarizes the causes of the project delays:

GOVERNMENT DELAYS THE PROJECT

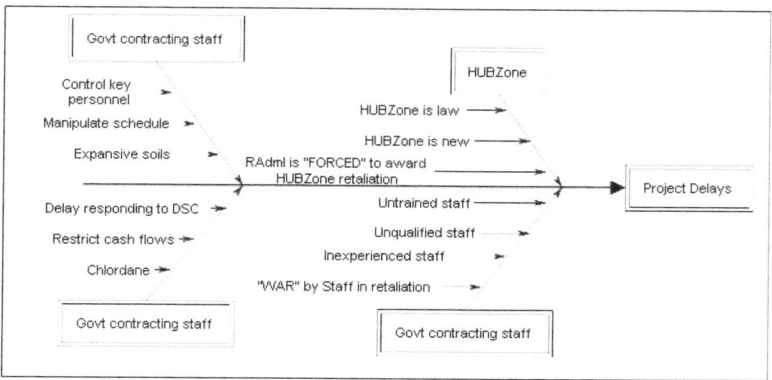

It is clear that the government contracting staff decided that the HUBZone contractor would receive the full treatment of deception and manipulation. The biggest hammers that they had were the control of the schedule, restriction of cash flow, control of key personnel and delays. These hammers would make the HUBZone contractor "putty" in their hands. The only values in the delays to the project are to deplete the float and to extend the contract completion date so that liquidated damages can be assessed against the HUBZone contractor. Delays on the project are used against the contractor and subsequently allow the restriction of cash flow. Illegally restricting the cash flow does not produce any value to the completion of the project. Its' only value is to cause destruction for the HUBZone business.

6

Restrict Cash Flow

The life of any construction project is the cash flow. A HUBZone contractor relies on the covenant of good faith and fair dealings for the simple principle of payment for work performed or materials provided. The HUBZone contractor can expect to be paid for services, products and materials provided for the benefit of the government. He can expect to be paid for the work and services provided in a prompt manner. The last thing the HUBZone contractor or anyone can anticipate is the restriction and control of the cash flow of the project. Actions to restrict the cash flow serve no purpose other than to control the HUBZone contractor and to destroy the financial stability of the HUBZone business.

The government's contract staff decides that they will hold retention on the project. This means they will start to restrict the cash flow and release the monies as they see fit which does not comply with law. However, the government is supposed to act in accordance with the rules and regulations of the contract. The Federal Acquisition Regulations (FAR) for payment is referenced in the contract. There are specific regulations concerning the use of "retainage" from payments. The FAR 52.232-5(e) requirements state:

"(e) Retainage. If the Contracting Officer finds that satisfactory

RESTRICT CASH FLOW

progress was achieved during any period for which a progress payment is to be made, the Contracting Officer shall authorize payment to be made in full. However, if <u>satisfactory progress has not been made</u>, the Contracting Officer may retain a maximum of 10 percent of the amount of the payment until satisfactory progress is achieved. When the work is substantially complete, the Contracting Officer may retain from previously withheld funds and future progress payments that amount the Contracting Officer considers adequate for protection of the Government and shall release to the Contractor all the remaining withheld funds. Also, on completion and acceptance of each separate building, public work, or other division of the contract, for which the price is stated separately in the contract, payment shall be made for the completed work without retention of a percentage."

Based on the above regulations it is clear that the government can retain funds from a progress payment where the progress is not satisfactory. And when the progress is substantially complete they can release the retained funds. For example if the pouring of sidewalks is behind schedule retention for that work would be expected. However as soon as the sidewalks are poured the work activity is substantially complete and the funds released. In principle this is fair and consistent. In this contract the HUBZone contractor is not treated in accordance with the regulations and the use of retention is used illegally. The events regarding the use of retention to restrict cash flow are astounding.

The earlier chapter regarding the manipulation of the schedule is a factor in the governments' justification for holding the retention. As described in the FAR the retention is held "*if <u>satisfactory progress has not been made</u>*", How would determination of satisfactory progress be made? The manipulation of the schedule did not allow the HUBZone contractor to show the government caused delays and the contract completion date could not be shown as delinquent. Yet the government decided that satisfactory progress had not been made when they decided in December 2003 to hold the first retention, **before** any real work started! Keep in mind that the demolition started in late December 2003. The government delayed the site work on the project by refusing to provide direction and response to the differing site conditions from the expansive soils. Retention is held throughout 2004 and by July 2004 the amount of retention held is in the range of $339,318.00. This is a significant amount of monies at a point of time in the construction where the project was in delay and the concrete slab work is starting up again. The progress of the project had been held up due to the lack of response by the government to address the differing site condition caused by the expansive soils. The project schedule is manipulated by the government and does not show the government caused delays for this time frame. How did the government justify the startup of retention when they were causing the delays? Further they controlled the schedule so their liability would not be reflected in the schedule.

It is also a critical point in time for the government because they had not approved the Project Manager that was hired in February 2004. The person hired was highly qualified and experienced; and the government contracting staff was unqualified and inexperienced. The government contracting staff is uncomfortable dealing with a highly qualified and experienced federal contracting project manager; however they continue to hold retention and restrict the cash flow. By July 2004 concrete slab construction will start at the HUBZone contractor's own risk because he cannot wait any longer for the government to make their decision on the differing site condition. **The government agrees to release $100,000.00 in retention if the HUBZone contractor will replace the highly qualified and experienced project manager.** This is a clear abuse of authority for holding the retention in the first place and then to blackmail the HUBZone contractor with monies that they already earned to control the management of the construction project. The HUBZone contractor is in a plight or fight situation and has no choice but to release the project manager. This action is unreasonable and shows the violation of the FAR for holding and releasing retention. In the July 16, 2004 correspondence the HUBZone contractor reports to the Resident Officer in Charge of Construction:

RESTRICT CASH FLOW

> *"This provides a written followup to our discussion this afternoon. In summary I have decided to replace the current Project Manager, N--- F----- effective July 16, 2004. The General Manager, W----- C---, will assume the responsibilities of the Project Manager during the interim until a suitable Project Manager has been employed and approved by the ROICC. Per our discussion and mutual understanding, the interim replacement is satisfactory and will meet the requirements to immediately release the $100,000.00 retention and to bring M____(HubZone Contractor) into compliance with the contract."*

The government continued to hold retention and was never clear why they were holding 10% of the progress payments in the first place since the contract completion date showed the project to be on time. It created a shortage in the cash flow and the HUBZone contractor had to resort to personal loans to continue funding the government's project. These loans are in excess of $6M and created a financial burden on the HUBZone contractor. According to the regulations as long as progress is made and the work activities are substantially complete the funds should be released; however that is not what happened. The government used the retained funds which is the HUBZone contractors' monies for completed work to require agreement to contract modifications that were inappropriate. The coercion of contract modifications under duress is a common practice with the government contracting staff on this project.

The HUBZone contractor encountered a fiber optic cable that was in an area that was not previously identified. The government took a considerable amount of time in trying to identify the owners, and the resolution to the presence of the cable. This delay affected the HUBZone contractor's off-site work and they submitted a claim for the delay. The ROICC decided to use the retention to blackmail the HUBZone contractor in releasing the claim and accepting a time delay that was inaccurate. The time impact analysis for the delay was never analyzed or evaluated by the unqualified and untrained government contracting staff. The HUBZone contractor filed a claim for the unresolved difference. The government discussed the release of $1.25M, a significant amount of monies that had been held between July 2004 and September 2005. The government requires the HUBZone contractor to rescind the claim and agree to sign a "bilateral modification" in exchange for the release of $1.25M. It must be re-emphasized that the retained monies belong to the HUBZone contractor since it is for work that had been completed and substantially complete. It is NOT additional monies for added time to the contract or to pay for increased cost of the work. This agreement is clearly blackmailing the HUBZone contractor with the funds that he has earned for work already completed. To place the plight of the HUBZone in perspective the September 2005 timeframe is the peak of production and the highest cost of the project's cash flow. There is no fight for the HUBZone contractor and he has no choice but to sign the illegal and improper contract modification under duress. The blatant disregard for the rules and regulations applicable to the retention, and to the covenant of good faith and fair dealings is shown in the handwritten meeting notes by the ROICC:

> **Agreed To**
> 1) ROICC Release $1.25M, retain $500k
> 2) ~~send~~ ROICC ltr rescinding claim
> 3) ~~sign~~ mod providing 75 calendar days (18 add'l) for FO cable making mod Bi-lateral.

Timing of the bribery and blackmail is a critical factor for the HUBZone contractor. By September 2005 the project is at its' peak in production, the site work is also in delay because of the identification of the chlordane contamination on the project, and the single largest pay request for the project was submitted in September 2005. The cash flow at this point means the project is fully manned by all of the

RESTRICT CASH FLOW

subcontractors and vendors. The payment due to the subcontractors and vendors is critical and releasing $1.25M in retention will mean those that did not get paid prior to September 2005 would be paid. What choice did the HUBZone contractor have but to comply with the wishes of the government blackmailer? The signing of the bilateral modification meant that the HUBZone contractor would have to agree to "full satisfaction and accord" for this issue. By all common sense the blackmailing of the HUBZone contractor is "duress" and certainly not legal.

The progress and history of the payment and retention for the project can be illustrated. The cash flow of the project paint the horror of the history of events. The following illustration provide a historical review of the retention held by the government, payments made by the government and the periods in time where the HUBZone contractor had to make personal loans to keep the project moving in a forward direction.

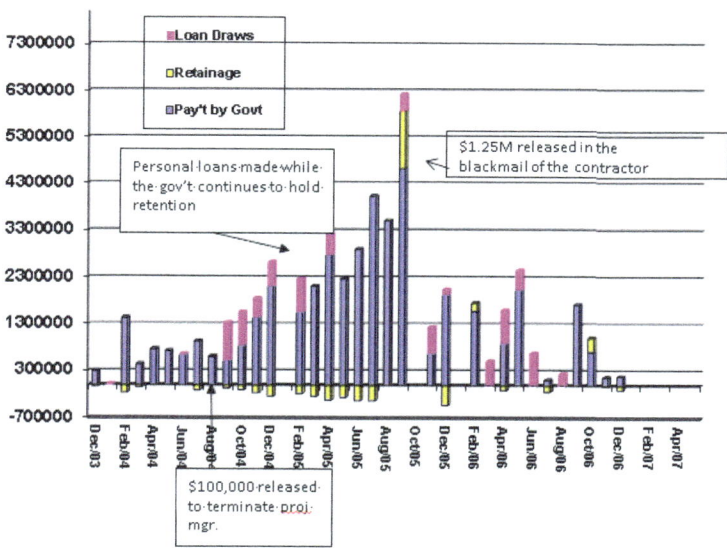

The above illustration reflects the personal loan draws and the final release of $1.25M during the peak period of the construction. The government directly impacted the cash flow of the project and caused a financial burden for the HUBZone contractor. In addition the government delays caused cost overruns for the project which became the added burden to the HUBZone contractor. The burden becomes so great toward the end of the project that the HUBZone contractor has to rely on the bonding company to assist with finishing the project. The project is being assessed 10% retention from December 2004 on and the onslaught of retention never justified.

The HUBZone contractor attempts to meet with the Congressional Delegation to get some assistance with the government's disregard for the regulations. The attitude and arrogance of the government's response to Hawaii's Senior Senator can be seen below:

-----Original Message-----
From: _____LCDR
Sent: wednesday, May 04, 2005
To: _____CIV
Subject: _____(HUBZone contractor) SOUNDBITES
>
> Sir,
> Here's some "vanilla" soundbites:

Gen _____(Senator Staffer),
As always, I appreciate the advance notice when one of your constituents is unhappy with business on MCBH. I looked over the information you sent, and I can understand why HUBZone contractor may be concerned. Their contract completion deadline is quickly approaching, and they may be feeling more pressure as the prospect of being assessed liquidated damages appears to be more of a certainty. Our local NAVFACPAC contract office keeps me very informed on this project, as we remain concerned about the progress and quality of the work. There are a lot of details in _____ (HUBZone contractor's) submission, but I wanted to comment on two things. **The practice of retaining 10% of the earned**

RESTRICT CASH FLOW

"work-in-place" is permitted in the Federal Regulations and customary whenever there is a serious concern about a contractor's ability to complete the project on time. I am confident that_____(HUBZone contractor) is not being singled out in this respect, as the decision to retain is taken very seriously by the NAVFACPAC contracting officer. *We all recognize the importance of cash flow, particularly in the case of a small business or HUBZONE contractor.* Regarding the fiber optic line, we recognize that this issue required some unexpected planning on the part of MCBH, _____ (HUBZone contractor), and NAVFACPAC. I am not able to discuss the details (do not believe that they have all been worked out), but the contracting officer will address whatever impact to _____ (HUBZone contractor), if any, is attributable to this issue and will adjust the contract appropriately.

>

> As for recommendations on how to respond to _____ (HUBZone contractor), certainly you could always forward these comments to NAVFACPAC for an official response. Although the work is on MCBH, NAVFACPAC, as our contracting agent, would be responsible to address these contractual concerns. However, as a practical matter, I recommend that your office just listen to these with concern for the record. *Certainly the unfortunate circumstances surrounding this contract have made this a very difficult road for* _____ *(HUBZone contractor), and we sincerely hope that his surety or other banking assets are able to assist him in his cash flow problems, at least in the near term.* At this particular time, I respectfully suggest that your office is not really in a position to arbitrate the situation or intervene on _____ (HUBZone contractor) behalf, as there are remedies within the contractual framework that are available to resolve the differing site conditions and other changes that may happen during the construction. Until all avenues for resolution have been exhausted with the contracting office and final contracting officer's

decisions been made, I believe that _____ (HUBZone contractor) could best help itself by continuing to make solid and deliberate progress on the required work to demonstrate a willingness and, more importantly, an aptitude to complete the job.
>
> *ViR,*
> _____*LCDR*
>>
DEF0444103

Cash flow is the life blood of the construction contract for the HUBZone contractor. Manipulating the schedule and using the inaccurate schedule to justify the illegal holding of retention severely restricted the cash flow on this project. The above email does not recognize the government's illegal and unreasonable behavior and the impact on the cash flow. The above email does express their spitefulness in regard to the cash flow issues i.e., "*Certainly the unfortunate circumstances surrounding this contract have made this a very difficult road for M_____, and we sincerely hope that his surety or other banking assets are able to assist him in his cash flow problems, at least in the near term.*" Throughout this book we see the implications and the spitefulness with the "circumstances surrounding this contract" and it is no secret that they are referring to the protest and the HUBZone requirements.

One of the greatest and most compelling characteristics of a small business is their endurance and the strength to move forward. They are too small to engage in time consuming rhetoric, or in long meetings to discuss nothing and resolve less. They make firm decisions, remain committed to their company and their customers, and they don't quit. The history of this project and the endurance and strength of this HUBZone contractor is a lesson for all. The HUBZone contractor draws all profit monies from other projects, drains savings accounts and secures personal loans to continue with the project even when the government has taken all efforts to cause destruction of the business. The project is completed in "spite" of the "forced" HUBZone contract

RESTRICT CASH FLOW

attitude and he clearly demonstrated the "aptitude to complete this job". The actions by the Navy to restrict the cash flow and the destruction of the HUBZone are incomprehensible. These actions lack logic and certainly does not address the covenant of good faith and fair dealings which serve as the basis for construction contracts. However, this is not the only atrocity of this project. The Commanding Officers for the Navy and Marine Base intentionally contaminate the housing project with carcinogens and limit the information to the residents. The HUBZone contractor cannot control the negligence and disregard for the quality of life for the military families. There are no justifiable or acceptable reasons for spreading contaminated topsoil with known carcinogens in the front and backyards of the homes of these young families.

7

Navy Contaminates the Housing Project

The pesticide was legally applied for many years and in 1988 the Environmental Protection Agency (EPA) banned the use of this pesticide due to the health effects of the product. Chlordane, heptachlor and heptachlor-epoxide are Group 2B carcinogens as classified by the International Agency on the Research for Cancer. The request for proposal and the pre-bid question informs the HUBZone contractor that the chlordane levels were lower than the EPA remediation goals and that no remediation actions were required.

More than halfway through the project in July 2005 the Navy directed additional soil samples to be tested for chlordane. The samples revealed that there was contamination of some areas of the project site and the stockpiles of dirt were contaminated with the carcinogens. The Navy specifications which are part of the contract documents provide the methodologies for handling the chlordane contaminated materials. The HUBZone contractor proceeded with following these specifications and notified the government officials of a differing site condition for handling the chlordane contaminated materials on the project. However, the government does NOT allow the HUBZone contractor to follow the contract but delays the project. The government is

NAVY CONTAMINATES THE HOUSING PROJECT

unresponsive resulting in a delay to the project from July 2005 to late December 2005. Further the government does not analyze the delay and the impact of the delays. The government simply adds the <u>impact</u> of these delays to the late completion of the contract resulting in liquidated damages being assessed to the contractor.

In late December 2005 the Navy issued a unilateral modification to the contract. This modification "directs" the HUBZone contractor. Although the HUBZone contractor did not agree with the contamination of the housing project the unilateral modification was issued by the Navy. Once the unilateral modification is issued the HUBZone contractor has no choice but to comply with the direction by the Navy, at his cost. The modification directs the HUBZone contractor to leave all of the contaminated topsoil that was spread prior to detecting the chlordane contamination in place. And the remaining contaminated topsoil piles will be used as topsoil and spread throughout the project. Despite the HUBZone contractor's many protests the work was completed. It is an undisputed fact that the contaminated topsoil was spread throughout the housing project and landscaping planted.

The atrocity is the decision to handle the contaminated stockpiles in a careless disregard for human health. The Navy's response to the chlordane contamination is to require the HUBZone contractor to produce contaminated topsoil. The contaminated topsoil was spread throughout the project and the landscaping planted. The State of Hawaii Department of Health (HIDOH) required that the contaminated topsoil be removed and that 18" to 24" of clean topsoil be placed over the contaminated areas of the project. The Navy arbitrarily decides that the HIDOH does not have jurisdiction at the marine base and ignores their direction. The action by the Navy creates exposure to hazardous substances. Their action allows the disproportionate risk of cancer to the infants and children and it can only be classified as criminal.

The Navy directs the HUBZone contractor to spread the contaminated topsoil throughout the project. Despite protests and attempts to bring public attention to this matter he must comply. He tried to fight

THE CONTRACT FROM HELL

the irrational and negligent actions of the Navy and failed. The following map shows the extent of the contamination throughout the project with grass. The red areas are the contaminated areas.

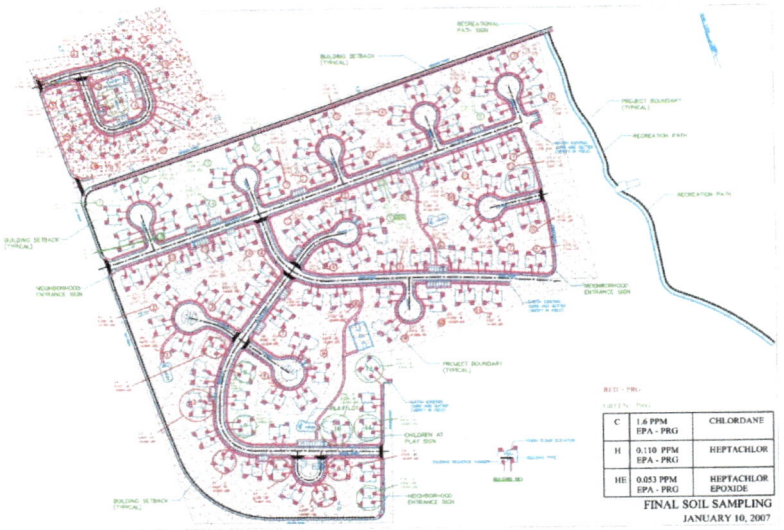

The HUBZone contractor must face the reality that the project will be completed with carcinogens spread throughout the project. The unsuspecting military families will have to live with this contamination. The proper handling of chlordane is specified in the contract documents and there is no reason for the government to interfere with the progress of this project to inject these additional and negligent actions, except to save money.

WHO WILL PAY THE PRICE? This project will expose the military families to known carcinogens. The chlordane, heptachlor and heptachlor-epoxide are spread throughout the project and lawns and landscaping planted. The government contracting staff delivers to their customer, the American Taxpayer, a contaminated housing project. There is no reason or rationale that can justify these actions, yet these conditions exist today and the military families are not aware of their exposure and risk.

In previous chapters we discussed the practices and dealings of large businesses and the government on these types of projects. The idea that the large business would submit a low bid and allow the government to manipulate the rest of the monies allocated by Congress provides for the inefficiency and inaccuracy of the initial request for the project to Congress. We find this to be a significant factor. The Navy knew from previous projects, specifically the residential housing project adjacent, to this project that chlordane contamination was present. As a matter of fact we discover that the Navy knew of chlordane contamination throughout the marine base prior to the award of this contract. The request for proposal for this project specifically stated that the chlordane was present and that the levels were below the action levels and that no remediation would be required. In July 2005 we find that this is not true. How will the Navy fund the initial inaccuracy and inefficiency of the request for proposal?

By delaying the HUBZone contractor and driving the assessment of liquidated damages the Navy can get the HUBZone contractor to pay for this inefficiency and inaccuracy. It is the only way because they already awarded the contract at its' full price of $48,000,000.00. The detected chlordane is a problem and the Navy concocts a way to declare the site safe, save some money and pass the cost to the HUBZone contractor.

You be the judge, is the contaminated housing project safe? The next chapter will discuss the assessment and the determinations that are incomplete and misrepresented. However, there is one outstanding fact that will weigh heavily on our minds. During the process to rationalize and justify the contamination of a residential housing project the Navy environmental engineers and managers are communicating with each other. The primary environmental engineer that promoted and advocated the use of the inaccurate Human Health Risk Assessment (HHRA) and chose to ignore the pollutant discharge to the environment testifies for the government. During his deposition he is asked while under oath if he and his wife with his newborn would live on this project and he would not answer. When asked if he would grow vegetables on these back yards and feed them to his family, he would not answer.

THE CONTRACT FROM HELL

A compelling story from a former spouse at the Kaneohe Marine Base describes a terrible history. This story from previous generations can be the story for future generations. Her story in her own words is shown below:

"Dear Mr. C____

I read your report how the military are building homes on dangerous ground. I have a story to tell you about my family and DDT that was used during the time my husband was stationed at Kaneohe in 1948 through 1950. The military furnished housing at Kaneohe, the housing unit was called termite village. During these two years the military sprayed the base daily with DDT, they had a mechanical device that was hitched to a jeep to spray with, in addition to spraying the island the housing unit issued DDT can sprays for the families to use inside the apartments to kill the cockroaches.

Is this the same area that the military approved the ground is safe for military families to live? My entire family including myself developed tumors and cancer, I had two children, I lost one with cancer, years later I lost my husband from toxic exposure, mercury and DDT combined, colon cancer, severe nerve damage. If I can be of any help to prevent the building of these home. Please advise.

I know the pain and suffering of toxic exposure. It may take years to effect the body.

Sincerely,

D_____ R___."

The Navy says it is safe—is it?

8

Contaminated Housing Project Is Not Safe

The Navy decided to conduct a human health risk assessment (HHRA) to justify the contamination of a 212 residential housing project for our military families. The actions to spread contaminated soils throughout the project will expose unsuspecting military families and their children to carcinogens. Low level pesticides in the front and back yards of the residents of unsuspecting military families and their children can be the cause of the unexplained illnesses experienced and it cannot be safe. The very nature of the human health risk assessment must include the scientific basis for such an assessment. There are many Executive Orders to ensure these assessments include the scientific and legal basis to ensure accuracy and effectiveness. Any effort to ignore these directives and regulations and to develop an ineffective HHRA only created unsafe housing and it saved money.

The atrocity of this project is the intentional spreading of topsoil contaminated with known carcinogens in the front and backyards of the ~50 acre residential project. Added to this atrocity is the intentional deception of the residents in these areas and the environmental contamination that results from contaminated topsoil throughout the project. The contamination of a residential housing project and the assumptions that are concocted to justify these actions is an on-going nightmare of the contract from hell. There is no dispute as to the fact that the housing project is contaminated with carcinogens. There are several issues:

1. The Navy decides that they will conduct a human health risk assessment (HHRA) to justify the contamination of the front and back yards of the residential units. The human health risk assessment does **not** meet the criteria for an acceptable assessment issued by the Navy, the Army Corps of Engineers for Dept of Defense (DoD) sites, and the Environmental Protection Agency (EPA). The applicable Executive Orders for these risk assessments are ignored. The Navy's HHRA is unacceptable.

2. The subsequent notification to the residents is modified to intentionally tell them ½ of the truth resulting in residents who are unaware of the carcinogens in their front and back yards and the exposures to themselves, infants and children.

3. The contamination of the residential site does not consider the pollution to federally protected waters and the environment. Protection of our environment and exposures to future generations is intentionally ignored. The Federal Water Pollution Act is violated and ignored.

4. Consider who are affected and who will be affected. This is a 212 residential housing project. The Navy's projection is that one family would only be exposed for a maximum of 6 years. This means 212 families will be exposed for 6 years resulting in a compounding of the exposure population every 6 years. How many infants and children will be exposed at a point in their life time when they will receive 50% of the cancer risk posed by this housing project? If these homes are around for another 50 years over a thousand families will be impacted. This action will affect generations to come.

CONTAMINATED HOUSING PROJECT IS NOT SAFE

The Human Health Risk assessment (HHRA) is supposed to be a scientific study using the best possible information and data. The most important role of the HHRA is to ensure the parents or public officials understand the possible human health risks from the environmental media. It is not intended as a means to save money or to extend construction contracts. The Navy scrambles in July 2005 to push the development of a haphazard and incomplete document that they call an HHRA by December 2005. The Navy's inadequate HHRA only evaluates the stockpile of soil and some contaminated sites it does not ensure that the housing project is safe. It does NOT address the conditions of the site and therefore cannot be representative of the unsafe conditions. The HHRA falls short of being an acceptable risk assessment.

We must expect the HHRA to address the minimum concerns for the exposure of carcinogens. The Navy's HHRA fail to answer all of the questions of a competent HHRA. The Environmental Protection Agency (EPA) defines acceptable human health risk assessments as:

"A human health risk assessment is the process to estimate the nature and probability of adverse health effects in humans who may be exposed to chemicals in contaminated environmental media, now or in the future.

To explain this better, a human health risk assessment addresses questions such as:

- *What types of health problems may be caused by environmental stressors such as chemicals and radiation?*

- *What is the chance that people will experience health problems when exposed to different levels of environmental stressors?*

- *Is there a level below which some chemicals don't pose a human health risk?*

- *What environmental stressors are people exposed to and at what levels and for how long?*

- *Are some people more likely to be susceptible to environmental stressors because of factors such as age, genetics, pre-existing health conditions, ethnic practices, gender, etc.?*

- *Are some people more likely to be exposed to environmental stressors because of factors such as where they work, where they play, what they like to eat, etc.?*

The answers to these types of questions helps decision makers, whether they are parents or public officials, understand the possible human health risks from environmental media."

What was assessed? The description of the Navy's HHRA memorandum states: *"This memorandum presents the results of a human health risk assessment performed on soil samples (i.e., __samples of stockpiled soil and in-place soil__) collected at the Replacement of 212 Family Housing Quarters site located at Marine Corps Base Hawaii (MCBH) in Kaneohe, Oahu, Hawaii."* The biggest concern with this HHRA is the fact that the assessment is conducted of the stockpiles of soil and some areas of the construction site **BEFORE** the contaminated soil is spread throughout the project. **Nowhere in the HHRA is there an assessment of the exposure to the families, infants and children once the contaminated topsoil has been spread throughout the project. Thus the representation for exposures is severely skewed.**

The assessment does not take into consideration the exposures after the contaminated materials are spread over the entire project which would reveal a more accurate and consistent assessment. The assessment only addresses the stockpiles of soil and some areas on the site. The HHRA is inaccurate and does not adequately assess the exposure pathways to humans. This cannot be safe.

Ignoring national policy and guidance. The Navy's HHRA fail to meet the criteria and guidance issued by various federal agencies. Although the communications and correspondence issued by the Navy repeatedly emphasize that their HHRA meet the USEPA guidance we find that this is **not** true. The Department of Navy Policy requires that the HHRA include interaction and concurrence with the regulators, contractors and stakeholders. For example, the Navy intentionally ignores any comments or input from a major stakeholder, the State of Hawaii, Department of Health. The Department of Defense (DoD) has guidance issued by the U.S. Army Corps of Engineers for DoD contaminated sites. The conduct of a proposed plan or statement of basis is prepared and made available to the public which explains the proposed action. At the very least input from the stakeholders is required and the Navy intentionally ignored the State of Hawaii and we note that there were no public hearings.

The USEPA guidance is not followed; however the Navy chose some guidance and ignored others. The most significant guidance ignored is the disproportional risk of cancer to the infants and children. The national policies established by Executive Orders are completely ignored! Executive Orders 12898, "Federal Actions to Address Environmental Justice in Minority Populations and Low-Income Populations", and 13045, "Protection of Children from Environmental Health Risks and Safety Risks", are not addressed in the Navy's HHRA. <u>The HHRA lack the scientific basis and compliance with national policy.</u>

The manipulation of numbers is not an assessment. The HHRA that is produced in December 2005 does not focus on the exposure assessment but set on raising the limits to allow the contaminated soil to be used on the project. The HHRA is biased and is used to raise the action levels or the EPA's preliminary remediation goals (PRG) to a level that is 20 times higher. The Navy's HHRA is not a scientific study to properly evaluate the exposures but a mathematical manipulation of the figures to save money.

For example, the EPA preliminary remediation guides (PRG) for chlordane at that time was 1.6 ppm and one of the factors used to determine this figure is the length of exposure. An exposure of about

30 years is used as an active lifetime exposure. Thus the intent is that an adult exposed to this level of chlordane, i.e., 1.6 ppm for a lifetime (~30 yrs.) would run a risk of one in one million for cancer. To simplify this would mean soil concentrations less than 1.6 ppm would not result in an increased risk of cancer of one in one million. The Navy modifies these figures by saying that the Marine families are only exposed for 6 years or no more than 2 tours of duty at the Kaneohe Marine Base. They arbitrarily extrapolate and decide that 6 years of exposure would allow raising the 1.6 ppm limit by a factor of 20 or 32 ppm. It is interesting that one of the higher soil samples is ~30 ppm and it does appear to be more than coincidental that their HHRA matches these numbers. The manipulation of the 30 years of exposure versus the 6 years produce a $1/5^{th}$ exposure or a factor of 20, and this alone is **not** an exposure assessment. (The factor of 20 is mathematically incorrect.)

This assessment does not allow for exposures from other bases where this same methodology is used, or for future construction in the same area with increased background levels of the carcinogen, or any other potential exposures. It completely ignores the pathways of exposure and the concentrations of such exposures. For example, how does this manipulation of the numbers reflect the exposure of an infant crawling around in a layer of dust with chlordane, heptachlor or heptachlor epoxide? The short answer is that it doesn't.

A significant issue with the Navy's HHRA is the fact that the manipulation of these figures does **not** address the exposures to infants and children. This is a relevant and key issue since the cancer risk to infants and children occur in the first two years of life. It is estimated by EPA that 50% of the cancer risk is received in the first two years of life. How does this fit into the equation above to allow exposures at increased levels for 6 years? IT DOES NOT! The significant lifetime exposure to the infants will be in the first two years because the families in these residential units are young marines and they are starting their families.

The Navy's assessment is made to allow the front and back yards of the residential units to be contaminated with chlordane. To put this into perspective the Navy's assessment allows chlordane levels 20 times higher than the EPA's PRG where the cancer risk assumption is also increased by a factor of 20. The acceptability of these numbers is unacceptable because cancer risks for only the soil concentrations is an incomplete picture. The HHRA does not include the increased cancer risk to infants and children which is ignored. The factors associated with a proper HHRA are manipulated and the Navy directs the HUBZone contractor to process the contaminated stockpiles and to spread the contaminated soil in the front and back yards of these residential units. The actual conditions created are never assessed properly. **Manipulating the numbers and ignoring the exposure to the infants and children does NOT make the contaminated housing site safe for the families.**

Sampling Basis is inadequate. The Navy's HHRA is based on an inadequate sample size for the area. They decided to use the soil sampling that was taken by the contractor to characterize the site for the construction work. The contractors' sampling was never intended to be used for a HHRA nor was there a proper determination made on the representative sampling that should occur. The contractors' sampling was purely a random sampling to determine the approximate size of the contamination. On a 50 acre site the Navy erroneously and conveniently decides that ~135 soil samples taken in the soil stockpiles and various site areas are sufficient for a HHRA. The State of Hawaii Department of Health (HIDOH) disagrees that the number of samples are representative and are concerned that the low number of samples will not include all of the risk. The HIDOH reviewed the Navy's assessment provided by the HUBZone contractor and they identify specific weaknesses in the assumption of the sampling data that is used in the draft report. The comments provided by the HIDOH are ignored; (1) some of the sample data was not included in the assessment; (2) not all of the contaminated stockpiles are considered in the assessment; (3) there is one hot spot that the government decides to remediate and the HIDOH requires additional sampling to clearly identify the other areas that may contain higher levels of chlordane.

The Navy disregards input and comments from the HIDOH. The Navy alleges that chlordane is everywhere because it was legally applied many years ago. Accepting this assumption then it must be concluded that a community wide approach to the handling of this kind of carcinogen is prudent. For example, handling of contaminated housing projects outside of the marine base should be handled in the same manner thereby keeping the population exposures relatively consistent. This is the purpose of the EPAs' preliminary remediation guidelines. However, the Navy in this case decided that their HHRA is acceptable and they disregard the comments provided by the HIDOH. The attitude or tone at the time is best reflected in their internal correspondence. One of the military managers asks the question, *"Is there a precedent or reason we would ask DOH to officially review the risk assessment when they have no jurisdiction?"* The response back is, *"I believe the precedent is that we not ask for DOH review when they have no jurisdiction."*

The idea that the Navy would conduct their HHRA without the input from the HIDOH is in itself a violation of Executive Order 11514, "Protection and Enhancement of Environmental Quality", which requires the Heads of federal agencies to work with the State and Local agencies to ensure protection of our environment. The Executive order requires:

"Heads of agencies shall consult with appropriate Federal, <u>State and local</u> agencies in carrying out their activities as they affect the quality of the environment."

The Navy's HHRA is based on an insufficient sampling methodology and it has been pointed out by the HIDOH. The Navy intentionally disregards this important factor in conducting their partial and biased HHRA. The basic definition of a HHRA includes representative sampling data and accuracy. The HHRA fails to meet the criteria of a human health risk assessment because it does not accurately estimate the nature and probability of the adverse health effects. <u>Based on</u>

CONTAMINATED HOUSING PROJECT IS NOT SAFE

the limited amount of information used the HHRA cannot say the site is safe.

Exposure Assessment: We find that the Navy's HHRA includes a section dedicated to exposure assessment. The exposure assessment is a summary of reference doses and slope factors, in other words a listing of scientific jargon. We did not find an actual assessment regarding the actual exposures (dose) that would be encountered. For example children and infants crawling on the floors and ingesting the dust, or dust buildup in the residential units that are completely sealed for air conditioning, etc. We also note that the exposure assessment did not take into consideration the consumption of vegetables or fruits grown in the yards of these residential units. A year later the Navy admits they did not consider the exposure from ingestion. Their internal correspondence states: *"The risk assessment we conducted to clear the site did not factor in plant uptake but just incidental ingestion."* It is not safe to underplay the exposure.

Pathways of exposures are ignored. The pathways of exposures are a significant set of factors when considering the human health risk assessment. These pathways are ingestion, inhalation, and absorption of the carcinogen by the human body. Careful consideration to the residential units and the exposure of these families to the exposed carcinogens must be weighed. Exposures in this assessment lack the evaluation of dust buildup in these sealed units for airborne dusts; the dust buildup in the units and the exposures to the infants and children as they crawl around the home; and the ingestion of the dust buildup as well as the vegetable consumption in contaminated gardens. It is not safe to exclude or to limit some pathways of exposure.

Inhalation pathway not properly addressed: The exposure from the airborne dust that is tracked into the sealed residential units will create an exposure in excess of the background levels. The EPA PRG showed an ambient air limit of 1.9E-02 ug/m^3 for chlordane, 1.5E-03 ug/m^3 for heptachlor and 7.4E-04 ug/m^3 for heptachlor expoxide which are NOT addressed by the Navy's HHRA. Note: ug = microgram or one millionth of a gram. The buildup of dust in the sealed air conditioned units will only increase over time resulting in an increase of exposure. The HHRA only assessed the stockpiles of soil and the points of contamination on the construction site. It did not address airborne exposures from the buildup of dust in the residential units. <u>Failing to address all of the pathways of exposure is not safe.</u>

Dermal exposure pathway is not properly addressed: Dust buildup in and around these homes will include the carcinogens. The most significant concern is the exposure of the infants and children as they crawl around and play in the dust buildup. Their dermal and ingestion exposure will be far greater than an adult. <u>This pathway is not addressed and it is not safe to improperly evaluate all of the exposure pathways</u>.

Ingestion exposure pathway is not properly addressed: Many families grow their own vegetables in their backyards. Without knowing the hazards of the carcinogens in their soil they will ingest contaminated vegetables and fruits. The HHRA did not address consumption of contaminated vegetables as admitted by the Navy. Internal correspondence shows that the Navy had not assessed this exposure pathway:

"The risk assessment we conducted to clear the site did not factor in plant uptake but just incidental ingestion."

Once the families occupy the residential units it is noted that many of them immediately plant vegetable gardens in their back yards. The Navy and the housing authority deliberately decide NOT to tell these families of the risk of consumption of contaminated vegetables from these gardens. In the development of a "fact sheet" for the residents the Navy drafts show that the vegetable gardens are an issue of conflict. The Navy Environmental Health Center who conducted the HHRA is trying to develop this "fact sheet".

"I've discussed this with the other NEHC Risk Communicators and Risk Assessors. We have shortened this fact sheet, and taken out much of the technical information based on feedback from the

CONTAMINATED HOUSING PROJECT IS NOT SAFE

MCBH personnel that we met with last week. There concern was similar to Captain G___'s—i.e., what will the 20 year old marine think? They wanted to have something to give people who ask questions about is the soil safe—a starting point to educate on chlordane in soil and encourage follow on questions if needed. That is how we came to this current version. They wanted to explain:

- *Chlordane was used legally by the Navy*

- *It's virtually everywhere*

- *There are no legal sampling requirements or maximum soil concentrations*

- *In a few cases, the Navy does sample and study—and follows USEPA guidance*

- *Health effect information for chlordane,*

- *Basic do's and don'ts to help people manage the situation (reduce exposure)*

- *POCs—Go to the housing office or your doctor for more information*

- *I was asked not to write this as a site specific fact sheet, but as a generic NEHC public health information sheet. The local personnel wanted to reference indirectly the risk assessment work and highlight that anything we do follows USEPA guidance and the 30 year exposure scenario*

I am willing to change or further simplify anything provided we don't try to act like there are no potential health effects from chlordane, because anyone doing a simple internet search will find this

THE CONTRACT FROM HELL

is not true. I've tried to put the health risks in perspective by discussing how exposure around the homes is much lower than those that have resulted in health effects such as occupational exposures. Please provide more information on which particular section or sections that need more simplification."

In response to the above email the Captain at NAVFAC PAC decides to water down the message on the ingestion exposures.

"the part about vegetable gardens is a non-starter. We just told them it was safe, but now we say it isn't. why can't we say following normally acceptable hygiene practice ... washing your hands before eating, washing fruits and vegs, things we should be doing anyway ... works here too."

The exposure pathway for ingestion of the contaminated vegetables from being grown in the contaminated soils is ignored and kept from the occupants. A year later the Marine environmental manager admits that the HHRA did not address the consumption of contaminated foods.

"The fact sheet suggests ways to avoid "incidental" ingestion through washing your hands and washing fruit/vegetables before consuming them. The fact sheet did not specifically address eating vegetables from a garden because the uptake issue is complicated and the understanding at that time was that vegetable gardens would not be allowed. Lt. Col L___ also had this same understanding.

The risk assessment we conducted to clear the site did not factor in plant uptake but just incidental ingestion. The standard consumption rate is 100 mg/day for children and 200 mg/day for adults. 100 mg is equal to about 0.0035 ounces by weight and about $1/10^{th}$ of ¼ of a teaspoon by volume. I do not have the expertise to correlate plant uptake with actual ingestion of pesticides so I will

CONTAMINATED HOUSING PROJECT IS NOT SAFE

need to defer to NEHC. NAVFAC has consulted with NEHC in the past regarding the di/no-dig policy and NEHC has taken the conservative stance that there should be no digging. They may recommend no vegetable gardens."

The housing project is occupied by 212 families with infants and children. The exposure from ingestion of vegetables grown in the backyards of these residential units is ignored. The Food and Drug Administration (FDA) issue limits for various food commodities. For example the contents of chlordane in foodstuff are limited by the FDA. The action levels for vegetables are 0.1 ppm. To keep this in perspective the EPA Preliminary remediation goals (PRG) or the Navy's action levels for this project were raised from 1.6 ppm to 32 ppm by the Navy's HHRA. This means they increased the FDA level by a factor of 20. Again using the Navy's method of manipulating the figures we can view the ingestion issues in similar fashion. Although they did not consider the ingestion of food from the gardens they inadvertently allow an increase from 0.1 ppm to 2 ppm! Increasing the limits of contaminated food stuffs to expecting mothers also means an increase or the introduction of the carcinogen to the unborn children. **The site is NOT safe and underplaying the facts and limiting the information/ precautions to the residents does not make it safe.**

Discharge of carcinogens to the environment is ignored. The project is contaminated with 6" to 8" of contaminated topsoil throughout the project. The contaminated soil will produce sediment over the years through rain, maintenance and other activities. The sediment will be discharged to the storm drains and discharged to the federally protected waters surrounding the marine base. This environmental discharge is ignored. The Federal Water Pollution Control Act (Clean Water Act) and Executive Order 11514, along with other local laws are violated by allowing the discharge of pollutants to the surrounding federally protected waters. The Executive Order requires federal agencies to:

"(a) Monitor, evaluate, and control on a continuing basis their agencies' activities so as to protect and enhance the quality of the environment. <u>Such activities shall include those directed to controlling pollution</u> and enhancing the environment and those designed to accomplish other program objectives which may affect the quality of the environment. Agencies shall develop programs and measures to protect and enhance environmental quality and shall assess progress in meeting the specific objectives of such activities. Heads of agencies shall consult with appropriate Federal, <u>State and local</u> agencies in carrying out their activities as they affect the quality of the environment."

The manipulation of the PRG numeric values does not address exposure to infants, children and toddlers. According to EPAs Guidelines for Carcinogen Risk Assessment, children receive 50% of their lifetime cancer risks in the first two years of life. **THE CANCER RISK TO THE INFANTS AND CHILDREN IS NOT ADDRESSED IN THE HHRA.** The construction project is completed by leaving contaminated topsoil in the front and backyards of the residential units. The occupants are young families many of whom will give birth to their infant children while living in these units. The exposure to infants and children are significant on the marine base. The HHRA issues are (1) the Navy did not consider the exposure of the carcinogens to infants and children as required by the USEPA Guidelines for Carcinogen Risk Assessments; and (2) the Executive Order that prohibit the exposure of infants and children to a disproportionate risk from environmental health and safety risks is ignored.

It is undisputed that the housing project contains contaminated topsoil with chlordane, heptachlor, and heptachlor-epoxide. These are Group 2B carcinogens as classified by the International Agency for the Research of Cancer (IARC). The use of contaminated topsoil spread over the yards of the entire housing project was directed by the Navy and it is an undisputed fact. The presence of the contaminated topsoil presents exposures to the residents, maintenance and utility workers

CONTAMINATED HOUSING PROJECT IS NOT SAFE

as described in the Navy's HHRA. However the exposure assessment does **not** address the disproportionate risk of cancer to early-life exposure. The Navy decides to ignore an Executive Order for the disproportionate risk of early life exposure to carcinogens. The Executive Order 13045 states:

Section 1. Policy.

> *1-101. A growing body of scientific knowledge demonstrates <u>that children may suffer disproportionately from environmental health risks and safety risks</u>. These risks arise because: children's neurological, immunological, digestive, and other bodily systems are still developing; children eat more food, drink more fluids, and breathe more air in proportion to their body weight than adults; children's size and weight may diminish their protection from standard safety features; and children's behavior patterns may make them more susceptible to accidents because they are less able to protect themselves. Therefore, to the extent permitted by law and appropriate, and consistent with the agency's mission, each Federal agency:*
>
> > <u>*(a) shall make it a high priority to identify and assess environmental health risks and safety risks that may disproportionately affect children; and (b) shall ensure that its policies, programs, activities, and standards address disproportionate risks to children that result from environmental health risks or safety risks.*</u>*"*

The housing project was intended to increase the quality of life for our military and these residential units constructed for the younger marines. A feeling of the age group of these residents can be seen in the Navy's attempt to address the residents. We know from internal correspondence that the Navy Captain for this effort is trying to finalize a public notice regarding the chlordane at the housing project and he categorizes the residents:

THE CONTRACT FROM HELL

> *"While I mean no disrespect to any of our Marines or their families, the fact is we will be reaching out to many Marines and spouses in the early 20s and in some cases barely out of high school."*

In my discussions with some of the military families I found that many of them are NOT *"barely out of high school"*. As a matter of fact they have college degrees and many of them are pursuing higher levels of education while raising a family. They are hard-working, dedicated, loyal mothers and fathers. They trust that the military would provide them with safe and healthy housing and they are not so ignorant or stupid that they would not understand that they are being exposed to carcinogens. The Navy got this one wrong.

The population of the residents consists of an age group in their early 20s and most of them are starting their families. The exposure assessment does not address the disproportionate risk of cancer resulting from exposure to the infants and children. It should also be noted that many of these families are starting to have their children and the assessment of exposure to the pregnant mothers are also not addressed. The contaminated vegetables and fruits discussed in the previous sections identify the exposure to the unborn children that must be addressed. Ignoring the high level of exposure to the infants and children does not make it safe. <u>The high level of exposure to the infants and children is inexcusable and it is not safe.</u>

The HHRA did not take into account studies, evaluations and risk assessments conducted by the scientific community regarding these pesticides. For example, a study conducted around 1977 and the report issued in 1982 PRIOR to the EPA ban for chlordane clearly addressed the concerns regarding exposures to military families in military housing then and in the future. "An Assessment of the Health Risks of Seven Pesticides Used for Termite Control" (1982 prepared by the Committee on Toxicology was not included in the HHRA. It is interesting that this risk assessment was prepared by the Board on Toxicology and Environmental Health Hazards Commission on Life Sciences. The risk assessment was contracted to them by the National

CONTAMINATED HOUSING PROJECT IS NOT SAFE

Academy of Science and the Office of Naval Research, contract no. N00014-80-C-0161. Ignoring the risk assessment that addressed the exposures to military families cannot be acceptable to anyone.

SUMMARY

The contaminated housing project is not safe. The Navy used an inaccurate, incomplete, and biased HHRA to attempt to show that the contamination of the housing project is an acceptable alternative to properly constructing the project. The HHRA is a poor justification for not providing a safe and quality housing area for the military families. Amidst all of the scientific mumbo jumbo the reality and the facts are simply:

1. The residential housing project was contaminated with carcinogens. The exposed topsoil provides exposure to the infants and children, adults and workers. There is no dispute that the Navy directed that contaminated topsoil be used in the front and back yard of these residential units.

2. The level of contamination is not treated in a manner to protect human health. The Navy's poor excuse for an HHRA and simply declaring the site "safe" is unacceptable. The assessment is inadequate, violates Executive Orders, Federal Law, and is highly questionable at best.

3. Regardless of whether the HHRA is accepted or not the facts are:

    A. The site is contaminated.

    B. The level of chlordane, heptachlor, and heptachlor-epoxide contamination is at least 20 times the acceptable levels by EPA.

C. The exposure to the infants and children were not considered; however we know that the EPA guides and the Executive Order requires the Navy to consider the exposure to infants to be higher. The Navy's HHRA increased the exposure risks to infants.

D. When considering the exposure to the infants the Navy erroneously raised the "acceptable levels" without adequately considering protective measures for the infants, and children. <u>This is particularly important when the fact that infants and children receive **50%** of their cancer risk in the first two years of life. The HHRA does not address this significant risk.</u>

E. The Navy manipulated the numbers to allow the raising of the remediation goals from 1.6 ppm to 32 ppm by changing the duration of exposure to 6 years. Raising the susceptible cancer risk to infants and children is **NOT** safe.

F. There is no consideration given to the ingestion of contaminated vegetables by the pregnant mothers, unborn children and the infants and children.

G. The contaminated site will result in pollutants being discharged to the federally protected waters surrounding the marine base. This is a violation of the Federal Water Pollution Act. The discharge of the hazardous substances throughout the base is not considered, i.e., the tracking and transferring throughout the base

4. The motivation for this atrocity can only be one thing, money. Somewhere along the line it was decided that the assumption of risk of exposure to the military families and the infants and the compliance with Federal Law or any Executive Order were

inconsequential when it came to the amount of money that is saved. The facts speak for themselves. A lot is said when the civil environmental engineer coordinating the HHRA and the acceptability of the project would not move into these units or allow his family to live there or to eat vegetables grown in the backyards of this project. Somehow they allowed their risk assessment to expose the military families, infants and children to a disproportionate risk of cancer. What are the cost savings and the cost of life?

Note: In 2014 a group of military families, representing over 100 military families filed a lawsuit against the private public venture (PPV) managing the housing. Military families, including their infants and children were experiencing unexplained illnesses. These illnesses appeared after they moved in to the housing at the Kaneohe Military Base.

It may not be safe but it saved money!

9

Cost of Contaminating a Housing Project

The Navy uses a poorly conducted human health risk assessment (HHRA) to risk away the risks caused by spreading carcinogens on the site. The only obvious motivation for conducting the incomplete and biased HHRA is the short sited perception that there is a cost savings. Since exposing the military families and their infants and children to the carcinogens in a flagrant and unsafe exposure is not logical, one has to conclude that this is the only reason. The obvious reason for the HHRA is the cost to remove the contaminated soils and replacing it with clean soils. The weighing of the cost savings versus exposing the infants and children to the carcinogens and polluting the environment is the battle. ***The cost savings won this battle.***

Using general ball park figures to examine the cost motivation for the HHRA we can come to some general conclusions that reflect the actions to save money; allow the exposure to the carcinogens; and pollution of the environment . There is a right way to have accomplished the work and then there is the Navy's HHRA way.

The right way:

1. The right way to have accomplished this work is to have the

COST OF CONTAMINATING A HOUSING PROJECT

HUBZone contractor follow the contract specifications for the handling of chlordane contamination that was approved at the time of the design and approval of specifications.

2. This would have required the HUBZone contractor to notify the State of Hawaii Department of Health and to handle the contaminated soils accordingly.

3. A representative sampling plan would have been developed for evaluation of the site and identification of the scope of the work to remove the contaminants.

4. The basic scope of work would have included a removal of the contaminated stockpiles from the site.

5. Once the contaminated stockpiles were removed from the site new clean topsoil for the project site would be required. Any hot spot contaminated areas could have been cleaned up prior to spreading the clean topsoil.

Cost of the right way: For the purpose of discussion the following conservative costs can be applied. The ball park figures are provided for the sake of discussion and an appreciation of the order of magnitude of costs. This is a project consisting of ~50 acres or 2,178,000 square feet. The housing footprints take up about 18% of the area, i.e., ~397,808 square feet. The roads, tot lots, sidewalks, curbs and gutters take up about 40% of the project site, or 871,200 square feet. The open areas for front and back yards are assumed to be ~908,992 square feet.

BALL PARK FIGURES TO DO IT THE RIGHT WAY	COSTS
The navy paid the HUBZone contractor about $260,615 to remove the excess soils from the project.	$260,615.00

THE CONTRACT FROM HELL

The open areas where clean topsoil would be required is ~910,404 square feet by 8" deep to cover the chlordane contamination. The cost of clean topsoil treated with compost is ~$37.00 per cubic yard. Or 910,404 sq. ft x 0.75 ft. = 454,496 ft³. divided by 9 cu ft/cu.yd x $37.00 per cu yd = $2,807,079.00.	$2,807,079.00
A rough estimate for trucking this amount of soils is $1,500,000.00 for the sake of discussion. It is assumed that an arrangement is made for the trucks to haul off the contaminated soil while bringing back clean soil thereby reducing this cost.	$1,500,000.00
Allowing for 3% overhead and 10% profit of the soil cost and the trucking.	$559,920.00
The ball park figures to address the chlordane contamination properly would be in the order of $5,127,614.00	$5,127,614.00

The atrocity—Risk away the risk and save money:

1. The construction site was initially characterized by using random sampling points to show the rough locations of the contaminated areas. This was not intended to be a representative sampling of the site. It would only provide an overview and it was insufficient to be representative of the area of exposure but it was used anyway for the Navy's HHRA. This is not a representative sampling data base for an assessment and cannot be used as an assessment to determine if the housing project site is safe. However conducting additional sampling would be costly and the decision to NOT conduct further sampling is a cost saving measure. It had nothing to do with the accuracy or the effectiveness of the assessment. Using a non-representative sampling base to determine the site is safe saves money.

2. The stockpiles of soils were sampled using a random sampling methodology and is no way representative of the contents of the stockpile. For example a sample was taken at the top, in the middle and the bottom of the pile. The stockpiles were large piles of soils in the order of 1,000 cubic yards each. To place

COST OF CONTAMINATING A HOUSING PROJECT

this in perspective the major stockpiles were two stories high. The proper assessment would have calculated/sampled the soil concentrations after it was spread in the front and back yards of the residential housing units. No such assessment has been produced. Again such an assessment would involve a cost and not conducting the assessment properly would save money.

3. The excess soils were removed from the construction project and taken to the local landfill. It cost the Navy ~$260,615.00 which they issued to the HUBZone contractor.

4. The contaminated stockpiles were then screened to remove the debris and weeds. Compost and fertilizer added and the contaminated topsoil was spread in the front and back yards of the residential units. The cost savings from not removing the contaminated soil from the site and replacing with clean soil is realized by the Navy.

5. The initial characterization of the site showed a small contaminated area and <u>could have been excavated and covered with clean topsoil</u>. This action alone would have completely eliminated the military family exposure to the carcinogens. However, the cost would include hauling in clean topsoil.

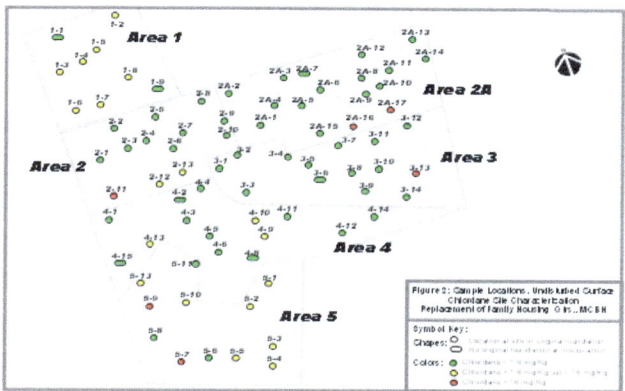

Site characterization BEFORE spreading the contaminated topsoil.

THE CONTRACT FROM HELL

6. The decision to spread the contaminated topsoil left the project in a catastrophic mess. By spreading the contaminated topsoil the area of exposure was increased throughout the rest of the project. The area of exposure is significantly increased but the cost of clean topsoil is saved. Exposing the families, infants and children and polluting the environment is cheaper than placing clean topsoil throughout the project.

After spreading the contaminated topsoil throughout the project

Kudos to the Navy for saving all that money? The total savings in ball park figures from the Navy doing it the wrong way is $5,127,614.00 – $260,615.00 that they gave the HUBZone contractor to remove the excess contaminated soils. A total savings of $4,866,999.00!!! Is it coincidental that the liquidated damages assessed to the HubZone Contractor was ~$3.7M? Is it worth it?

What is the cost of a child's life? Is the savings of $4,866,999.00 worth the life of one child, or the contamination of the environment for future generations? The population of exposed families is staggering and not addressed by the HHRA. Consider that 212 families

COST OF CONTAMINATING A HOUSING PROJECT

are exposed every 6 years per the Navy's projection. This means 212 families will rotate every 6 years and the population compounded. If there are 2 infants per family then the infant population is 424 every six years. In one generation of 50 years there will be 8 rotations and ~3,392 children exposed to an increased risk of cancer. This project is not acceptable. This increased risk is infuriating to the military families and cannot be compared to any dollars.

The intentional contamination of the housing project left the contaminated topsoil in a place where the sediment is washed into the storm drains and ultimately into the federally protected waters surrounding the marine base. The environmental fines for polluting carcinogens in federally protected waters can be in the several millions of dollars. How do we measure the impact of discharging carcinogens into the ocean and the impact to the marine growth and the fish and marine life? A good question is whether or not it is acceptable for the government to pollute the federally protected waters and get away with it because the State of Hawaii Dept of Health does not have jurisdiction? The impact to the environment, the marine growth and marine life is not measureable in dollars and cents.

How do we determine the cost of the exposure? We will have to wait until someone contracts a disease or is affected by the exposure before a case can be made. In the meantime many generations will be exposed to the carcinogens and their lives impacted without their knowledge. Despite the rules and regulations that are in place the atrocity of these residential units occurred. The disproportionate risk of exposure to carcinogens for infants and children was ignored and the health risks for leaving carcinogens in the front and back yards of residential units are "risked away".

It is somehow acceptable to the Navy to control the information provided to the occupants and mislead them regarding the carcinogen contamination. We are sure that the EPA's human health risk assessment was never intended to be a cost saving measure to "risk away" work that needs to be accomplished to protect our military families and their children. The intentional disregard of the elements to conduct a proper human health risk assessment is ignored and we are unable to stop them. What is the cost to our children and future generations? We will not be able to put a price tag on our children and the future generations.

What was the real cost to the HUBZone contractor? The chlordane contamination was detected in July 2005 and the Navy's human health risk assessment (HHRA) not completed until December 2005. The HUBZone contractor had to suffer the 6 month delay from July to December. The delay is ~180 calendar days and the Navy issued a 63 delay change order. The HUBZone contractor does not agree with the HHRA and attempts to get the Navy to properly address the carcinogen contamination. These efforts are futile and the HUBZone contractor is given direct instructions to spread the contaminated topsoil throughout the project. The decision to spread carcinogen contaminated topsoil throughout a military family housing project was based on the money saved with a high disregard to human health and protection of the environment.

There seems to be a concern that there may be more costs for this project and the HUBZone contractor is inundated with delays and allegations that will add to his costs. In addition to the previous delays of the project the government decides that the roof installation for the 106 buildings that were already completed and accepted are now not acceptable and they issue a unilateral change order for $399,000.00. As the units are completed the final inspections of these units are delayed for months at the HUBZone contractor's costs. Additionally a $290/day per unit liquidated damages are assessed resulting in a $3.7M assessment against the HUBZone contractor. The Navy saved a lot of money and also passed on these costs to the HUBZone contractor.

SUMMARY

It is obvious that money drove many of the decisions that were made in this project. The initial delays to impact the HUBZone contractor's performance to the extension of the contract completion date we can see the motivator for the delays, restriction of cash flow, etc. The costs

COST OF CONTAMINATING A HOUSING PROJECT

are used to make up the initial inaccurate and incomplete request for proposal which has a domino effect in creating changes to the contract. The HUBZone contractor has no way of knowing that money is an issue with the federal government and that they will be going after him for added costs created by the government. The costs that clearly belong to the federal government, i.e., the chlordane contamination, are "risked away" by a poorly constructed human health risk assessment. We wonder if the cost of a life for the carcinogen exposures, pollution of the environment, the costs added to destroy a HUBZone contractor, and the perceived costs savings by the Navy is worth it.

Is this legal?

10

Violation of Laws

The Navy's attempt at a human health risk assessment becomes the tool to save money and results in the increased risk of cancer to the infants, children and military families. The Navy contends in their correspondence internally and externally that they are completely legal. The complaints filed with EPA, the State of Hawaii Department of Health and the Hawaii congressional delegation are disregarded because of these contentions. The military families are exposed daily to an increased cancer risk. Does this look legal to you?

The legality of the Navy's actions can only be determined through litigation. The Navy is a federal agency and will continue to contend that their actions were completely legal. On that note we should examine the extent of the legalities and let the courts decide later. The Navy contends the following:

- Chlordane was legally applied and it is all over the place.

- The State of Hawaii Department of Health does not have jurisdiction on the marine base.

- The Navy's human health risk assessment employs and complies with the EPA guidance and the project is safe.

VIOLATION OF LAWS

- The Commanding Officer for the marine base approved the action to contaminate the housing project.

Chlordane was legally applied. The Navy incorrectly assumes that the chlordane was legally applied and therefore there are no regulations or exposure controls are needed. There are discrepancies in their assumptions. The Navy alleges repeatedly that the chlordane, heptachlor and heptachlor epoxide were pesticides that were legally applied. This distinction is critical because it exempts them from having to meet the requirements of the Comprehensive Environmental Response Compensation and Liability Act (CERCLA). Specific requirements of the environmental act would be required, for example the National Contingency Plan (NTP) or the Resource Conservation and Recovery Act (RCRA). There is no doubt that the pesticide was legally applied many years ago prior to the EPA ban of this product.

However, once it is excavated and spread out over a large area then it cannot be classified as being "legally applied". The Navy's contention is convenient because it allows them to handle the contaminated site in any manner that they deem acceptable without having to involve the public stakeholders or regulators. It is their belief that it allows them to expose military families to these carcinogens at a higher risk. 40 CFR 302.3 defines *release*,

> "*means any spilling, leaking, pumping, pouring, emitting, emptying, discharging, injecting escaping, leaching, dumping or disposing into the environment (including the abandonment or discarding of barrels, containers, and other closed receptacles containing any hazardous substance or pollutant or contaminant)…*".

The decisions to intentionally contaminate the front and back yards of these housing units meets the definition of "*…dumping or disposing into the environment*" of the chlordane, heptachlor and heptachlor-epoxide. These contaminants are listed as hazardous substances in 40 CFR 302.4.

> *1 acre = 43,560 ft²; Assume 20 acres or ½ of the project consist of the front and back yards that are open to the residents; 20.9A x 43,560 ft²/A = 910,404 ft² x 0.75 ft(8"of contaminated soil) = 682,803 ft³ for the project. 1 ppm = 0.0000624 pds per ft³. 32 ppm x 0.0000624 pds/ft³/ ppm x 682,803 ft³ = 1,363 pds.*

The CERCLA regulations require that 1 pound or more of a release to the environment be reported and treated under the CERCLA regulations. In our ball park estimates of the volume of contaminated topsoil we show the open areas to consist of 6" to 8" of contaminated topsoil throughout the open areas of the project or ~682.803 ft³ the weight of 32 ppm of chlordane for this area would be ~1.363 pounds. This release was never reported by the Navy as required by the regulations.

The Commanding General approving the contamination of the housing site is justified by their improper interpretation of the regulations and laws. The justifications states, *"DOH's cleanup goal is guidance; there is no law specifying an acceptable level of chlordane at housing construction sites. Since the chlordane was legally applied in the past to housing foundations to prevent termite infestation, DOH will not challenge our recommended course of action."* Excavating and exposing the chlordane contamination throughout the site is a release by definition and NOT complying with the CERCLA requirements is illegal.

It is all over the place. The Navy contends the chlordane is all over the place because it was widely used. If we assumed that this is a correct statement then the exposure to the occupants of the housing project should be the same as the rest of the community. The exposure to the chlordane outside of the base should be equivalent to those inside the marine base. Control and construction of housing projects should meet a "community-wide" goal to ensure the exposures are proportional. The State of Hawaii Department of Health has the jurisdiction in the state to control the remediation of chlordane at housing projects.

VIOLATION OF LAWS

They follow the EPA, Region IX requirements and guidance for the control and remediation of chlordane throughout the state.

The Navy decided that the State of Hawaii Department of Health did not have jurisdiction and they disregarded the concerns expressed by the state. Federal agencies are required to comply with Executive Orders issued by the President. Executive Order 11514, "Protection and Enhancement of Environmental Quality" requires the navy to:

"Heads of agencies shall consult with appropriate Federal, State and local agencies in carrying out their activities as they affect the quality of the environment. [Section 2(a)]

"(c) Insure that information regarding existing or potential environmental problems and control methods developed as part of research, development, demonstration, test, or evaluation activities is made available to Federal agencies, States, counties, municipalities, institutions, and other entities, as appropriate." [Section 2(c)]

The Navy's HHRA pollutes the environment and raised the cancer risk for the military families. The National Environmental Policy Act (NEPA) requires an environmental impact statement (EIS) to be prepared prior to the contamination of the housing project. An EIS was not prepared. It should be noted that an EIS would require public comment and resolution. The Navy failed to meet the requirements of the NEPA thereby side stepping the requirements for public comment. The handling of the contaminated housing project is not consistent with the community efforts to remediate and control the exposure to chlordane. The Navy's assumption that the State of Hawaii Department of Health did not have jurisdiction is unacceptable and not in accordance with law and regulation. Keep in mind that the Navy rushed the HHRA between July 2005 to December 2005 which means there is no way they could have complied with the NEPA.

The Navy asserts that their human health risk assessment employs and complies with the EPA guidance and the project is

safe. Once the chlordane is discovered on the project site the contract specifications require that the HUBZone contractor comply with the Federal and State regulations. EPA has established preliminary remediation goals (PRGs) to identify "triggers" for more study and evaluation of contaminants. There is no doubt that chlordane, heptachlor and heptachlor-epoxide are hazardous substances and they have been classified by the International Agency for Research of Cancer (IARC) to be Group 2B carcinogens. The PRG tables that are provided by EPA include the precautions on the use of the tables. The Navy's HHRA does not address all of the exposure pathways, appropriateness of using chronic toxicity values to evaluate childhood exposures, etc. The EPA guides for use of table clearly outline these precautions:

> *"The Region 9 PRG Table combines current human health toxicity values with standard exposure factors to estimate contaminant concentrations in environmental media (soil, air, and water) that are considered by the Agency to be <u>health protective of human exposures (including sensitive groups), over a lifetime.</u> Chemical concentrations above these levels would not automatically designate a site as "dirty" or trigger a response action. However, exceeding a PRG suggests that further evaluation of the potential risks that may be posed by site contaminants is appropriate. <u>Further evaluation may include additional sampling, consideration of ambient levels in the environment, or a reassessment of the assumptions contained in these screening-level estimates (e.g. appropriateness of route-to-route extrapolations, appropriateness of using chronic toxicity values to evaluate childhood exposures, appropriateness of generic exposure factors for a specific site etc.).</u>"*

The HUBZone contractor is stopped from following the contract specifications. The decision is made to conduct a Navy human health risk assessment (HHRA) to allow the contaminated soils to be placed throughout the project. The HHRA is the tool and the justification to allow this atrocity. We discussed how the HHRA is incomplete, biased and unacceptable to declare the site safe. The Navy goes out of their way to ignore the Executive Orders that are applicable to the HHRA and violate Navy policy and directives.

Executive Order: Executive Order 13045, "Protection of Children from Environmental Health Risks and Safety Risks" provides for the identification and assessment of the risks to the infants and children. The Navy's HHRA ignores this Executive Order which requires:

"Therefore, to the extent permitted by law and appropriate, and consistent with the agency's mission, each Federal agency:

(a) shall make it a high priority to identify and assess environmental health risks and safety risks that may disproportionately affect children; and

(b) shall ensure that its policies, programs, activities, and standards address disproportionate risks to children that result from environmental health risks or safety risks."

Executive Order: Executive Order 11514, "Protection and Enhancement of Environmental Quality" requires federal agencies to, *"a) Monitor, evaluate, and control on a continuing basis their agencies' activities so as to protect and enhance the quality of the environment. Such activities shall include those directed to controlling pollution and enhancing the environment and those designed to accomplish other program objectives which may affect the quality of the environment. Agencies shall develop programs and measures to protect and enhance environmental quality and shall assess progress in meeting the specific objectives of such activities. Heads of agencies shall consult with appropriate Federal, State and local agencies in carrying out their activities as they affect the quality of the environment."* We know that the Navy did not coordinate their efforts with the State of Hawaii and that the HHRA does not protect or enhance the environmental quality of the housing project.

Executive Order: Executive Order 12898, "Federal Actions to

Address Environmental Justice in Minority Populations and Low-Income Populations" require federal agencies to ensure that identifying and addressing disproportionately high and adverse human health or environmental effects of its programs, policies, and activities on minority populations and low-income populations. The Navy's HHRA adversely affects the environment and results in a disproportionate risk of cancer to the low-income populations of our military families.

Executive Order: Executive Order 12088, "Federal compliance with pollution control standards" assigns responsibilities to heads of agencies for ensuring that all necessary actions are taken for the prevention, control and abatement of environmental pollution with respect to federal facilities and activities. One of the laws listed include the Federal Water Pollution Control Act which is violated by allowing the discharge of pollutants to the federally protected waters.

Federal Water Pollution Control Act: The Clean Water Act prohibits the discharge of pollutants to the waterways and is administered by the State of Hawaii Department of Health. The State of Hawaii Department of Health has jurisdiction and enforcement of these regulations. The Navy's HHRA ignores the pollutant discharges to the storm drains to the federally protected waters surrounding the marine base. The Hawaii Revised Statute (HRS) 342D states:

HRS 342D-1 Definitions: ""Person" means any individual, partnership, firm, association, public or private corporation, <u>federal agency</u>, the State or any of its political subdivisions, trust, estate, or any other legal entity."

*""Water pollutant" means dredged spoil, solid refuse, incinerator residue, sewage, garbage, sewage sludge, munitions, chemical waste, biological materials, radioactive materials, heat, wrecked or discarded equipment, rock, sand, **soil, sediment**, cellar dirt and industrial, municipal, and agricultural waste."*

""Water pollution" means:

VIOLATION OF LAWS

(1) Such contamination or other alteration of the physical, chemical, or biological properties of any state waters, including change in temperature, taste, color, turbidity, or odor of the waters, or

(2) Such discharge of any liquid, gaseous, solid, radioactive, or <u>other substances</u> into any state waters, as will or is likely to create a nuisance or render such waters unreasonably harmful, detrimental, or injurious to public health, safety, or welfare, including harm, detriment, or injury to public water supplies, fish and aquatic life and wildlife, recreational purposes and agricultural and industrial research and scientific uses of such waters or as will or is likely to violate any water quality standards, effluent standards, treatment and pretreatment standards, or standards of performance for new sources adopted by the department."

One of the elements of an adequate HHRA is the impact of the exposure to the environment and the impact to the surrounding areas. The Navy's HHRA does not address the chlordane, heptachlor, and heptachlor-epoxide contamination that is left on site and discharged to the storm water system. The discharge of the contaminated sediment to the federally protected waters surrounding Kaneohe Marine Base is a violation of the Hawaii Revised Statutes that are applicable to federal agencies. Chlordane, and heptachlor are hazardous substances by definition. Both meet the requirements to cause bodily harm if inhaled, ingested or absorbed by dermal exposures. EPA has banned the use of chlordane since 1988; the Food and Drug Administration established levels of chlordane and its by-products to not exceed 300 ppb and in animal fat and fish not to exceed 100 ppb. Notification to EPA is required if 1 pound or more is released to the environment. A temporary guideline by the National Research Council indicates that 0.005 mg/m^3 should be the maximum amount allowed in the air of military housing. **The Navy's HHRA does not address these requirements for the control of the chlordane contamination on the housing project.**

The Navy HHRA does not meet the requirements of the agency: There are a number of policies, directives and requirements issued by the Department of Defense and others regarding human health risk assessments. The Navy's HHRA does not meet these requirements and are not consistent with the intent to protect human health. The following is a listing of these requirements:

- U.S. Army Corps of Engineers, "Environmental Quality Risk Assessment Handbook, Volume 1: Human Health Evaluation". The basic concepts of the human health evaluation are not followed in the Navy's HHRA:

  "1.4.1 Basic Concepts. The fundamental principles of good science and quality entail the thorough understanding of: (a) site chemical data; (b) an understanding of site related and background risks; (c) physical, chemical, and toxicity information associated with site chemicals; (d) fate and transport of site chemicals; (e) intake and extent of absorption; (f) the dose-response relationship of site chemicals; (g) uncertainties and limitations of the derived risk estimate; and (h) the best approach to characterize risk objectively."

- U.S. Army Corps of Engineers, "Guidance for Addressing Chlordane Contamination at Department of Defense Sites". The Navy HHRA fail to meet most of the requirements provided for Department of Defense sites.

  "b. Generally speaking the major components of response processes can be summarized as described below.

  (1) The suspected chlordane release is discovered. Notification occurs consistent with regulatory requirements. **[This does not occur.]**

VIOLATION OF LAWS

(2) An assessment is made to confirm whether a chlordane release has indeed occurred and whether additional action may be required. This is called a CERCLA Preliminary Assessment or RCRA Facility Assessment. If risk is considered acceptable, no further response action is taken. For example, if there is no pathway for chlordane exposure, further action may not be needed. If further action is necessary, the investigation proceeds to the next stage. [**The risk assessment is not acceptable.**]

(3) A CERCLA Remedial Investigation/Feasibility Study or RCRA Facility Investigation is conducted to define the extent of the contamination, evaluate risk, and assess alternatives for minimizing risk. Various alternatives for protecting human health and the environment from the chlordane are identified. Alternatives, for example may be 1) conduct no action; (2) remove exposure pathways by providing barriers to chlordane exposure; (3) impose land use restrictions to prevent exposure of sensitive receptors; or (4) excavation and disposal of areas elevated above cleanup levels to minimize overall concentrations. Each alternative is evaluated to determine whether it will be protective of human health and the environment and whether it will comply with regulatory requirements. Those alternatives that meet these threshold criteria are then screened based on implementability, cost, and effectiveness. Further detailed evaluation of retained alternatives eventually lead to a "preferred remedy". [**The spreading of contaminated topsoil does not fit into the acceptable remedies discussed above.**]

(4) A "Proposed Plan" or "Statement of Basis" is prepared and made available to the public which explains the proposed action. [**No public input.**]

(5) Responses to public comments are prepared and a formal decision document is signed. [**No public input.**]

(6) The remedy is designed and implemented." [**The spreading of contaminated topsoil does not fit into the acceptable remedies discussed above.**]

- The Department of Navy policy, "Conducting Human Health Risk Assessments Under the Environmental Restoration Program." (Ser N453E/1U595168, dtd February 12, 2001. This policy requires and emphasizes interactions and concurrence among the Navy project team, regulators, contractors and stakeholders. The Navy's HHRA ignores the community and they incorrectly assume that the stakeholders, i.e., the State of Hawaii, does not have jurisdiction. The screening, and data evaluations with the exposure pathways are specific and the Navy's HHRA does not meet the requirements of this policy.

SUMMARY

This chapter scratched the surface of the rules, regulations and laws that are violated by the Navy's HHRA and their subsequent actions to intentionally contaminate a housing project. Although astonishing this history of non-compliance with the laws and regulations is not new. Throughout this contract we have seen non-compliance and two federal judges decide that the actions of the Navy are arbitrary and capricious and not in accordance with law and regulation. When the Navy does not comply with the requirements of the contract, and when they disregard the law and regulation, who is accountable and who can help?

11

The Hubzone Contractor Is Alone

From the beginning it is difficult to comprehend the rationale for the government's actions. The HUBZone contractor is in a constant state of conflict with the government on almost anything and everything. Things like the submittal of a simple and important project schedule are the common documents that the owners and the contractor should review continuously. The HUBZone contractor is informed from the very beginning that they are new to government contracting and that they lack the knowledge and experience to perform this project. In their condescending manner they inform the HUBZone contractor that if he cooperates with them they will help him "through" this project. He is reminded that NAVFAC Hawaii/Pacific has never lost a protest prior to this contract.

We now know that the government contracting staff did not have the qualifications, training or experience to administer this contract. Not one of the government contracting staff members had any experience with administering a design-build project of this size, complexity and dollar value. This HUBZone contractor had completed complex multi-family residential construction projects for at least 25 years. He is experienced and qualified and demonstrated the completion of custom residential units with a market value in excess of $1,000,000.00 each.

THE CONTRACT FROM HELL

Another fact to consider is the continuing construction projects that were on-going in the middle of this nightmare with the government. Here is a list of projects that was completed or on-going during the 2003 to 2007 timeframe:

No. of Units	Award	Completion
126 Residential units	Nov 2005	June 2007
30 Low income apts	Dec 2005	Jan 2007
126 Residential units	June 2004	June 2006
84 Residential units	March 2004	March 2006
24 Residential units	Dec 2004	May 2006
32 Low income apts	Dec 2003	Jan 2005
20 Low income apts	Dec 2002	Dec 2003
74 Residential units	July 2003	Aug 2004
44 Single Family homes	Dec 2001	May 2003
168 Residential units	May 2002	May 2004
212 Gov't Residential units	Sept 2002	March 2007
940 Residents	TOTAL	

The HUBZone contractor was in the progress of completing a total of 728 residential units not including the 212 residential units for the government. The total work load for this HUBZone contractor at the time was 940 residential units! The government's project of 212 residential units represented 22% of his workload. Between 2002 and 2006 the average annual workload with the 212 project was 235 residential units per year. Not one of these projects was late or over budget. No one on the government staff had any experience or qualifications that came close to this level of workmanship, management, and coordination. It seems that the government contracting staff would have benefitted from partnering with a contractor of this expertise.

By late 2004 the government project had been delayed and the cost to the HUBZone contractor was increasing. The site subcontractor had already been terminated because they could not afford the losses of the government's delays. The HUBZone contractor managed to route the profit monies from the private projects to support the losses caused by the government. As the delays on this project continued, and the costs escalated the HUBZone contractor had to dig into his personal savings and personal loans to finish the project. This is the result of the effort of the government to drive the HUBZone contractor out of business.

In January 2005 the HUBZone contractor informs the Small Business Administration (SBA) that it is voluntarily removing themselves from the small disadvantaged business program because of their financial success. This could have been the government's spin to relate how the government awarded a $48,000,000.00 and allowed a small disadvantaged business with a HUBZone certification to graduate to the ranks of a large business. However, the opposite is equally true where the award of the $48,000.000.00 contract to a small disadvantaged business with a HUBZone certification was destroyed by the government's bad faith and unfair dealings.

While the improper and illegal actions are in progress, the HUBZone contractor finds himself in a fight for life. He has to fight to keep his head above water and to finish the project. What actions can he take to put an end to this madness or at least attempt to mitigate the damage caused by the government?

The HUBZone contractor made every effort to work with the government contracting staff. The government has no incentive or motivation to ensure a successful project with the HUBZone contractor, after all the Commanding Officer for NAVFAC Hawaii/Pacific views this to be a "forced HUBZone award." The contracting officers have no experience on a project of this size and complexity. The construction management engineer and the construction engineering technician are working against the HUBZone contractor's project management staff whenever and wherever they can. The person in charge is the Resident Officer in Charge of Construction (ROICC). We now know that he had no experience or qualifications to administer a design build project of this size and complexity. The President of the HUBZone contracting company meets with the ROICC personally and as often as possible to attempt problem resolution. None of these actions work as a matter of fact the individual responsible for the blackmailing of the retained funds is the ROICC. It is the same person that blackmails the HUBZone contractor into releasing the highly qualified project manager from the project in exchange for a release of $100,000.00 of the contractor's money. He is the same person that blackmailed the HUBZone contractor into releasing a claim and signing a bilateral contract change knowing that the time impact of the change was insufficient to address the time lost. This blackmailed deal resulted in a release of $1.25M.

The HUBZone contractor tried to move the issues up the chain of command to the Operations Officer and Executive Officer in the Naval Facilities Command for Hawaii and Pearl. He meets with them and informs them of the problems and the behavior that is costing time and money. He asks for resolution and provides recommendations for resolution. Each time he is given a half-baked answer that does not address any of the project issues. It is frustrating and he quickly recognizes that the higher in the chain of command he proceeds the less response he will get. He requests a meeting with the Senior Executive for the Command and the Rear Admiral does not respond. He requests meetings with the Commanding General of the base and staff who will be the recipients of the completed project, i.e., the customer, and it is denied.

The HUBZone contractor proceeds with following the Navy protocols and submits fraud, waste and abuse complaints. The complaint is sent to the Department of Defense and it is referred back to the Command. These are investigated half-heartedly by the same Command. And not surprisingly they find that there is no fraud, waste or abuse of authority.

The HUBZone contractor proceeds to solicit assistance from the Small Business Administration (SBA). He is referred to the SBA Advocate who works for the Navy and they are of no assistance. We now know that the SBA Advocate for the Navy views the HUBZone program as social welfare programs mandated by Congress. The contractor seeks assistance from the Governor and any other agency that will meet with him. None of these agencies can or will assist.

The HUBZone contractor seeks assistance from the Congressional Delegation in Hawaii. The retaliation for seeking assistance from the Congressional Delegation is blatant and a disregard for his rights to communicate with the Congressional representatives from the State. A summary of the actions and reactions regarding contacts with the Congressional Delegation is provided:

- In December 2004 the HUBZone contractor met with a Congressman and invited him to tour the project so that he could see the progress and quality of the work being performed. The ROICC was invited but declined to accept the invitation for the tour. On December 22, 2004 the Congressman invited the Base Commanding Officer to attend the tour. Upon completion of the tour the ROICC called and chastised the HUBZone contractor for inviting the Base Commanding Officer on the Congressional tour.

- As a result of the contact with the Congressman the following actions immediately followed:

    A. Non-compliance notices were issued. Nine of these notices were issued between January 4 to 11, 2005. It is blatant that 41% of the total non-compliance notices for the contract are issued in a two week period following the contact with the Congressman.

    B. The alternate Quality Control (QC) Manager was preparing to continue work during the Christmas holidays. The ROICC revoked a previous approval for the alternate QC Manager to work during this period because he exceeded

THE CONTRACT FROM HELL

his 30 day period as the alternate. The HUBZone contractor lost 4 working days as a result of this decision.

C. Although the Congressman offered his services to serve as a facilitator in the resolution of disputes or to improve communications the Navy did not respond. In an interview with the local newspaper the Congressman refers to the HUBZone Contractors' plight as the "contract from Hell".

- In response to a staffer for the Senior Senator in Hawaii, Honorable Daniel Inouye, the Navy responds to a request by telling them that they are wasting their time. Their response in essence informs the Senior Senator in Hawaii that they will be destroying one of their constituents and there is nothing the Senator can do about it. In an email response to the Senator's Staffer the Navy states:

"The practice of retaining 10% of the earned "work-in-place" is permitted in the Federal Regulations and customary whenever there is a serious concern about a contractor's ability to complete the project on time. I am confident that HUBZone contractoris not being singled out in this respect, as the decision to retain is taken very seriously by the NAVFACPAC contracting officer. We all recognize the importance of cash flow, particularly in the case of a small business or HUBZONE contractor. Regarding the fiber optic line, we recognize that this issue required some unexpected planning on the part of MCBH, M_____f, and NAVFACPAC."

The above response refers to the illegal use of retention. As stated they deny everything. The email then tells the Senator's Staffer that they will destroy the HUBZone contractor:

THE HUBZONE CONTRACTOR IS ALONE

> HUBZone contractor protested unfair award to large business.

> *"Certainly the unfortunate circumstances surrounding this contract have made this a very difficult road for _____ (HUBZone contractor), and we sincerely hope that his surety or other banking assets are able to assist him in his cash flow problems, at least in the near term."*

> "Surety or other banking assets"? Threat to destroy HUBZone contractor

The government acknowledges that they are hurting the HUBZone contractor's cash flow and that it is important. They respond by telling the Senator's Staffer that they hope the contractor can hold the financial burden of the project or the surety will have to step in. There is no doubt that as of May 2005 they know they will be ruining the financial capability of the HUBZone contractor. They now proceed to tell the Senator's Staffer how to react to the communications from their constituent because the Senator **cannot** do anything:

> *"At this particular time, I respectfully suggest that your office is not really in a position to arbitrate the situation or intervene on M_____'s behalf, as there are remedies within the contractual framework that are available to resolve the differing site conditions and other changes that may happen during the construction."*

Who you gonna call? The government is not accountable and will continue to deny-deny-deny that there is a problem and continue with inappropriate, illegal, wasteful and costly actions. It is a futile situation and the HUBZone contractor is left on his own to fend for himself. The plight of small businesses conducting business with the government is a story of the bully and the victim. The process allows the intolerable actions to continue at the HUBZone contractors' expense. There is no <u>accountability</u> in the long history of <u>fraud, waste and abuse of authority</u> and there is no help for the small business. This is the contract from Hell.

The concentrated efforts to raise the issue of unsafe housing for military families continued from 2006. The Navy's press releases and responses were always the same. The housing is safe. Bringing attention to the unsafe housing before anyone is affected was difficult and continues to this day.

12

The Contract from Hell

The title of this book comes from a news article printed by a local business news organization. The article describes the project, the plight of the HUBZone contractor and quotes a U.S. Congressman,

> *"They have had to fight from the beginning—It's been the contract from hell for them." The Congressman also stated, "This is not a fly-by night company—their owner is a hard-boiled guy who has been through some tough contracts. But he'll tell you, frankly, that this is the one that takes the cake."*

The contract from hell. The story of this contract from hell includes the full gambit of a rogue agency, the horrors of incompetent and unqualified people administering a $48,000,000.00 design-build contract, the abuse of authority to intimidate and coerce the HUBZone contractor, the outrageous, intentional, and atrocious contamination of the housing project and pollution of the environment. Add to this the fact that the HUBZone contractor does not have access to anyone or any organization that can or will help. The Small Business Administration advice to the HUBZone contractor is to "document" everything. The Navy's Small Business Advocate tells the HUBZone contractor the same thing. It is noted that the Navy's Small Business

Advocate views the HUBZone program as a "social welfare program" for small business. Why continue the work? Where do you go for help when the contract from hell is in progress?

Plight or Fight of the HUBZone: The plight or flight decisions that arose almost daily became a survival for the HUBZone contractor. Small businesses are used to making tough decisions and it is what makes them creative, innovative, strong and decisive. This project destroyed a strong, well reputed construction company in Hawaii; but it did not destroy the owner.

Once the onslaught started why continue? First of all the onslaught was not obvious in the beginning. The covenant of good faith and fair dealings is a common rule and practice in the construction industry. It is completely irrational to assume that the federal government agency will not act fairly and in good faith. The priority in the beginning of any construction project is to develop a sound plan and schedule for the execution of the work. Much of the energy and money is spent in moving in that direction. Very little, if any, thought is given to the strategy for defending against an onslaught of fraud, waste or abuse of authority. The assumption that you are dealing with the federal government and that there is an inherent vein of honesty and fairness is not an uncommon one. Construction project management prime order is to resolve problems and to move forward. Although the HUBZone contractor and staff did not understand the motivation for the actions by the government to delay the project, to manipulate the schedule, to control the project management staff, etc. they were fixated toward problem resolution. They did not consider the Navy's overall strategizing to default the HUBZone contractor from the beginning. The project started and all efforts to move forward are the goals of the day for the contractor.

Secondly, the HUBZone contractor is not one who gives up. Failing to get a response or to gain cooperation or to move forward meant that he needed to find someone of authority who would work with the HUBZone contractor to finish this project. Efforts to meet with anyone and everyone up the chain of command, agencies outside of the Navy to assist, the Congressional Delegation, etc. became almost a full time effort. Responding to the constant barrage of allegations, misrepresentations, and misinterpretations was a project manager's nightmare. The option to give up and to let the bonding company take over the project or to let the Navy have someone else assume the project is not a consideration for this HUBZone contractor. It became clear by late 2004 that the Navy was out to wreak havoc with the contractor's cash flow, progress on the project and to delay the completion date to impose liquidated damages. This HUBZone contractor does not give up because of his principle—his signature is on the contract.

Thirdly, this HUBZone contractor conducted business in Hawaii for 25 years and he built a large number of residential units. His policy and his ethics are in his integrity. He views the construction contract as a total commitment to complete a project. In over 25 years he has not walked away from a project without completing it. His integrity and character is based on his signature on the contract that he is committed and will finish the project no matter what. These kinds of ethics are rare and the commitment to finish is the kind of ethic that is found in small businesses. In spite of the obstacles, and the strategizing to terminate him for default the government could not stop him. He finished in spite of their efforts. It is interesting to note that in August 2004 after the government denied the differing site condition claim for the expansive soils they had conducted a secret analysis for the default. If they defaulted the HUBZone contractor it would take anywhere from 672 to 1149 days to complete the project, if they were lucky. In other words their efforts to default the HUBZone contractor were not efficient or practical.

It has been established that the Commanding Officer viewed this to be a "forced" HUBZone contract and that the Navy SBA advocate viewed the small disadvantaged business programs as *"social welfare programs"*. The SBA administers another small disadvantaged business program known as the 8(a) program. The certification is given to qualified small disadvantaged businesses with the intent to provide them with a preference for federal contracting in their completion with large businesses. The 8(a) program is one of the small disadvantaged business programs that are required by law.

In a separate 55 housing project constructed at the same marine base the project had to be awarded to an 8(a) contractor. The HUBZone regulations and the protest by the HUBZone contractor caused a stir and in 2004 the 55 housing project had to be rebid because the large businesses would not bid on the project. Their fear was that the HUBZone contractor would beat them again. The government changed the solicitation from a design build contract to a bid build construction project and awarded it to an 8(a) contractor. The small business finds themselves in the same boat as the HUBZone contractor. The government is resentful that the project had to be awarded to a small business and they set out to destroy the small business. After the initial startup of the project it became obvious to the 8(a) contractor that no matter what he did he would not succeed and that the Navy was out to destroy his business. This is also a construction business with a 25 year history and it represented all of the owner's assets and lifelong work. The restriction in the cash flow and the delays left him in a plight or fight situation and he had to walk away from the project allowing the bonding company to takeover. The Navy successfully destroyed another small business and the success of 25 years of hard work. The destruction of small businesses by unqualified and incompetent contracting staff is an astounding fact of life for the government agency.

As a small disadvantaged business what course of action is available when the contract from hell is initiated? Every small business and every lawmaker must understand that the good faith and fair dealings principle of contracting is a <u>duty</u>. Once this duty is breached and there is no accountability there is no place to go for help. The small business is doomed. The arrogance, incompetence and the willing to violate any law, rule and regulation without fear is a devastating element of this contract. Executive Orders, Federal Acquisition Regulations (FAR), Federal Water Pollution Act, etc. are laws that apply but ignored. The HUBZone contractor is intimidated by an agency that recognizes no authority or regulation. Will he expect the federal court to recognize his right to justice and fairness?

The process of filing a claim and having it denied and the process to file a claim in the Court of Federal Claims is time consuming and extremely costly. We are sure the government includes that factor in their decision-making. It is rare that a crippled small business will be able to fight back and tolerate the years of stalling and discovery. The attorney cost alone is cost prohibitive unless there is a strong commitment for justice and fairness. This commitment must come from others supporting the HUBZone contractor. The bank and the sureties must get behind him and support the fight for justice. The inequities and incompetence of the contracting staff is well recognized by the bank and sureties and they support the claim filed in the Court of Federal Claims.

The inequities continue throughout the claim. Any effort to stall and drag out the legal battle is employed by the government. Any efforts made by the HUBZone contractor to settle are met with strict opposition and a lack of fairness or negotiation. They simply deny any offer and leave the table. The attitude by the government is that they will continue the fight indefinitely until the HUBZone contractor cannot afford to continue. The fairness of a decision by the Court of Federal Claims will most likely be appealed and the process extended to drive the legal cost to the HUBZone contractor.

The concept of fighting for what is right for this HUBZone contractor and all other small businesses are clear. The decision to fight depends on the strength and character of a small business owner and the faith that right will prevail. The decision to fight must include an overwhelming premise that the accountability and rightful actions of our courts will prevail when the actions are illicit and unfair.

13

Sins of the Navy

How will the government explain their actions to the Judge in a Court of Federal Claims? This will be the third Federal Judge hearing about the illicit actions of the government contracting staff. We find that the government's defenses and the actions following the filing of the claims are consistent with their earlier illicit and unethical actions against the small disadvantaged HUBZone contractor.

In March 2007 the HUBZone contractor filed a request for equitable adjustment for the delays on the project. In response, the government debars the HUBZone contractor from government work. One must wonder what would have happened in 2005 or 2006 if the HUBZone contractor filed a request for equitable adjustment as the government continually requested. An early debarment would have crushed the efforts of the HUBZone contractor in 2005 or 2006. It is not a secret, the debarment is designed to cripple the HUBZone contractor so that he cannot continue to work and support the claim against the government. The debarment affects the HUBZone contractor's ability to perform State contract work and occurs **without** an adequate investigation and hearing. In other words the debarment is unfair and arbitrary.

The government decided to withdraw the debarment action during the hearing when they were having a difficult time justifying their unreasonable conduct. The actions of the government are not in accordance with law/regulations and in this case the Judge's opinion is that their actions are "arbitrary and capricious". This is the second Federal Judge to find the government's actions to be illicit. The Judge hearing the restraining order filed by the HUBZone contractor issues the following statement immediately prior to the government withdrawing the debarment action, she states:

> "And so to the debarment conclusion, I would think might be properly termed arbitrary and capricious. But I'm not going to do that today on your request."

By November 2007 the HUBZone contractor has no other choice but to file a claim in the Court of Federal Claims. The discussions, what little there were, resulted in the Navy denying any claims or any responsibilities for any delays or cost over runs. The costs for the claim are adding up and each month of discovery and depositions adds to the legal costs. These costs are significant and in order for the HUBZone contractor to proceed with the claim there are a number of considerations:

- The amount due on the loans made to keep the project moving while the government delays continued is a financial burden. The HUBZone contractor must keep the banks from moving forward and foreclosing thereby putting the company out of business. Note: If the company is out of business the claim is void because there is no "entity" filing the claim. It is therefore to the government's benefit to delay the claim, to prolong the process, and drive the legal costs upward.

- The amount due to the Sureties for completion of the project adds to the financial burden. The HUBZone contractor must satisfy the Sureties for the monies that were paid out to finish the project.

- The attorneys' fees and legal costs, e.g., cost of depositions, travel, per diem, etc. The HUBZone contractor must convince the attorneys to continue the fight for the claim and aid in bearing the cost of some of the litigation.

The claim against the government is a large and significant claim. What will convince the banks, Sureties and attorneys to support the cost of the fight? The answer is simple—*everyone believes the injustice of the events and they believe there will be justice on the day of trial.* The bank, Sureties and the attorneys believe in the strength of the claim and they must believe in the justice system of our country. The strength of the claim is supported by **many** and it is the only way the claim can progress toward a trial.

The HUBZone contractor makes an offer for mediation in an effort to settle the claim and in February 2009 a mediation session is conducted. The mediation is scheduled for two days. On the first day the government makes an unreasonable offer which is considered by the HUBZone contractor and a counter offer presented. <u>The government terminates the mediation.</u> This is not a surprising turn of events and it is consistent with the way the contract was administered. The government presented its' position and it is "my way or the highway". There is no partnership or team work or even a fair and honest negotiation. The only purpose of agreeing to mediation is to drive the legal costs as high as possible to defeat the HUBZone contractor.

The process of filing a claim for this project gives us access to the correspondence and the attitude, and illicit activities that went on behind the scenes. The HUBZone contractor did not know of the plans to destroy the HUBZone business. It leaves the HUBZone contractor in a state of confusion. Why is the government contracting staff being defensive and obstructive? The basic premise of any construction contract is the covenant of good faith and fair dealings. Both the owner and the contractor assume that the completion of the project to meet schedules, quality, budgets and safety are high priorities for both parties. The "partnering" of both sides to achieve the common goal of project completion and the turnover of badly needed and high quality homes for our military families is the goal. Without this elemental and critical covenant the project cannot proceed without losses and the destruction of the HUBZone business. We now know that the covenant of good faith and fair dealings was not in the priorities for the government from the beginning and that it had been replaced with a strategy to ensure that this HUBZone and future HUBZone companies would not be in a position to compete against the desired large businesses with the Navy. The Navy clearly did NOT want to award to another "forced HUBZone" contractor.

The government hires an expert to evaluate the claim and to provide a defense for the claim. Not surprisingly the expert uses the schedules produced and controlled by the government contracting staff to base his time impact analyses (TIAs) and the determination of the delays. There are several key things to remember about the schedule which the government expert ignores:

A. The scheduling software is required by the government and the specifications require a network analysis be used. This means the government and the HUBZone contractor must work on the schedule updates jointly and in agreement with each other as the project progresses. <u>This never happens because there is no covenant of good faith and fair dealings.</u>

B. The specification requires monthly meetings to discuss changes in activities, and impacts to the schedule. <u>This does not happen and the accuracy of the schedules purposely sabotaged.</u>

C. The specification requires the fragnet for change modifications to the contract to be conformed, i.e., the HUBZone contractor and the government contracting staff agrees which activities are impacted by the event(s) and the changes made accordingly. <u>The HUBZone contractor never received any conformed fragnets from the government or approved use of any fragnets</u>

<u>that the HUBZone contractor provided resulting in erroneous schedules.</u>

D. In essence the schedule became a document the government contracting staff manipulated to hold retention, to improperly rate the HUBZone contractors' performance, to restrict cash flow, and to prepare for future litigation. It had nothing to do with completing the project in a successful manner.

The government expert decided that the delays are attributed to the HUBZone contractor. The total delay to contract completion is 685 days. The government expert asserts that 549 days are accounted for by the government issued modifications which leaves 136 days attributable to the HUBZone contractor. He inadequately justifies his conclusion by:

- Performance issues by the site contractor that had to be terminated.

- Delays caused by the qualified project manager that was later terminated in exchange for a release of retention.

- Delays by the fencing contractor.

- Delays due to adverse weather and the concrete strike.

- He hints that there was $2.2M in rework; however the contractor never claimed for these costs.

Without addressing the true occurrences that impacted the schedule an analysis of any type is erroneous. The elements of the government expert's report are questionable and weak since he cannot address the missing delays and impacts to the schedule required by the contract. The government contractual violations are never addressed by the court or anyone else.

The government defense against the claim is to (1) find errors in the claim to charge the HUBZone contractor with "fraud"; and (2) to show that the project schedule reflects the delays to be the fault of the HUBZone contractor. The Defense Contracting Audit Agency (DCAA) is contacted by the Navy and an audit is requested. This audit is conducted over a period of approximately 1 year with no findings of fraud. The government hires an expert to evaluate the project schedules and determine who is at fault for the delays. As discussed above we see that the government expert's opinions are based on the government controlled and manipulated schedules.

The events covered in prior chapters are significant events; however there are the day to day events that continued throughout the project. The HUBZone contractor and staff lived through the constant criticism and degradation of their morale. An egregious example is illustrated by the government's allegations and accusations that the HUBZone contractor had the worst safety program that they ever saw. We already established that none of the government contracting staff had the experience, qualifications or training to make such an outrageous accusation. The fact of the matter is that this HUBZone contractor was one of the first general contractors to receive the Hawaii Occupational Safety and Health Achievement Recognition Program (SHARP) award; and that at no time throughout the project did their injury/illness rates exceed the national average for general contractors in this category. The SHARP award was based solely on the safety program that was in place at this project. Yet the government would insist that the HUBZone contractor enforce the requirement to wear a hard hat even when the plumber is working under the kitchen sink.

The quality of the workmanship and the final products is undisputed and it is noted that the government or their expert does not bring up quality issues. The residential units were completed and families occupied these units almost immediately. The warranty work on these units was minor and there were no significant workmanship or quality issues during the one year warranty period. Despite the government's efforts to sabotage the HUBZone contractor's performance he produced high quality homes for the Marine and Navy families. The undisclosed exposure of carcinogens to the military families are not an interest for the court.

The HUBZone contractor continues with his fight and proceeds with the claim in the Court of Federal Claims. The trial is conducted in parts and after the second part of the trial the HUBZone contractor makes an offer to settle. The government does not counter or negotiate. Their comments essentially inform the HUBZone contractor that they will appeal any decision by the court and a final decision will take about another 2 years. This means more legal costs to the HUBZone contractor. It is unlikely that the HUBZone contractor will see justice. The system itself will run him out of money and the decision will be unheard.

SUMMARY

The government contracting staffs' mantra of schedule, quality, and safety are only tools used to delay and harass the HUBZone contractor. This mantra is laughable because none of the Navy's contracting personnel on this project was trained, experienced or knowledgeable enough to administer and evaluate the schedule, quality or safety. The proof is in the pudding—there were no significant safety or quality issues on this project. And they controlled and manipulated the schedule.

The government's expert uses the government manipulated project schedule to show time impact analyses that attribute delays to the HUBZone contractor. He does not do any time impact analyses associated with the government caused delays or anything related to the 549 days where the government issued modifications. The expert relies on a general statement that these were concurrent and weather delays. We note that he does not analyze the impact of these delays to the subsequent work activities or to the project schedule as a whole.

The government expert cannot address the issues of impact to the work activities or to the project schedule because there is no accurate schedule that can be used to produce such an analysis. The government contracting staff ensured that the project schedule was not accurate from the beginning and used the schedule to mitigate government caused delays and to use up the float. The government caused delays in the last phases of the contract is caused by the chlordane contamination and the overzealous inspections by the "WAR" declared by the government inspector to delay the turnover of the residential units. It is obvious that these delays are aimed at final assessment of liquidated damages, ~$3.7M, to mitigate the government caused delays.

At the time of the certification for the HUBZone the small business concern is focused on completing the application and the certification process. Who or how will they be informed of the risk involved? Is it worth risking the loss of a solid 25 year business? What can be done to protect the small businesses from the government? Where do they go at the time they are being treated unfairly? Who do they go to? What authority exists to arbitrate or settle disputes of a project that is headed for destruction? Perhaps the Federal Acquisition Regulations (FAR) or the laws of the land need to address these issues. Since the government operates in a fully autonomous mode no one is held accountable and there is no way to prevent or stop an onslaught like this from occurring. The HUBZone law, the SBA rules, the FAR clauses, etc. are all dependent on the basic principle of good faith and fair dealings. This is a good concept but we can see that it doesn't work and there is no course of action for the small business until their demise.

The accountability for violating the good faith and fair dealings in the construction contract is a significant issue that must be addressed. However, the atrocity of this project is the intentional contamination of a housing project resulting in the disproportionate risk of cancer for exposure to the infants and children. There is not enough money saved to justify such a negligent and irresponsible action. The impact to the environment and future generations by the contamination of the federally protected waters with carcinogens is another significant horror that cannot be explained. There are others affected by this story and it is without an end. Who will tell the military families they are exposed to carcinogens every day and who will help them when they have to deal with the results of the disproportionate cancer risk to their infants and children?

This is truly the contract from hell.

14

Court of Federal Claims Decision

This is a David and Goliath case where a small disadvantaged small business has to fight for the right to be treated fairly and equitably by government officials. The Court of Federal Claims (CFC) erroneously assumes the contractor's intent to file the claim and fight the fraud, waste and abuse of authority is based on the *litigation based contractor* but the Judge fails to see the need for fair treatment and protection of the public's trust. The CFC decision in this case allows government officials to continue in bad faith or abuse of their authority. It is a violation of the public trust and it is a "win" for Goliath and allows future unfair and abusive contract administration. It is a license to kill business.

We take exception to the CFC's characterization of the HubZone Contractor's judgment and effort to file the claim and to fight the blatant and obvious violation of rules, regulations, laws and the presumption of good faith and fair dealings. We hope it is an aberrant judgment because it is the HubZone Contractor's **right** to bring this atrocity to the attention of the CFC and the public. It should be noted that the HubZone Contractor does **not** benefit financially by filing this claim and fighting for righteousness and fairness. He is supported by many others because they recognize the atrocious illegal actions by the government officials. The banks, sureties, subcontractors, attorneys, consultants, and vendors were NOT paid when the project was completed. Any award for damages will result in payment to those who were owed monies for the completion of the project and their participation in the filing of the claim. The HubZone Contractor makes NO MONEY, and his business, savings accounts, personal properties, and years lost are destroyed. The CFC's characterization that he is a *litigation based contractor* implies that he will receive a windfall is wrong and it is inappropriate.

> "It is from numberless diverse acts of courage and belief that human history is shaped. Each time a man stands up for an ideal, or acts to improve the lot of others, or strikes out against injustice, he sends forth a tiny ripple of hope."
>
> Robert Francis Kennedy quotes (U.S. attorney general and adviser, 1925-1968)

The Court of Federal Claims (CFC) relies on the presumption of good faith by government officials to justify their malicious and illegal behavior. The presumption of good faith is based on the public's trust that government officials will act in good faith in the performance of their duties. We trust government officials daily and we rely on the sacred honor of this trust by the government officials.

The actions and behavior of the Navy government officials to bribe the contractor into hiring their friends, or to bribe the contractor with the release of funds held in retention in exchange for signing inaccurate and improper modifications, or to hinder and hamper the contractor to terminate his contract are the kinds of actions that violate the public's trust.

The essential element of the presumption of good faith requires the public to trust that the government officials are well trained, experienced and accountable for their actions. The public trust that they will perform their jobs so that their duties and good faith are met. It presumes that the government officials will not act in a manner that

COURT OF FEDERAL CLAIMS DECISION

violates the rules, regulations, specifications of the contract and the laws. The assumption of good faith by the public's trust does not allow government officials who perform in an arbitrary and capricious manner or not in accordance with law/regulation. In this case the government officials are incompetent and they violate the public's trust by failing to perform their duties in accordance with the rules, regulations, specifications of the contract and the laws. At least two federal judges rule that the Navy official's actions are arbitrary, capricious and not in accordance with law/regulation.

The CFC ignores or missed the important duty to protect the public's trust and to ensure the elements for the presumption of good faith is preserved. The court issued a decision on December 9, 2011, four years after the claim was filed. The court decision is a shock and a real eye opener for contractors. The precedent that the government officials can violate the contract, act in bad faith, unfairly, fraudulently, and abuse their authority and be protected by the presumption of good faith is not known to contractors. Although this precedent is set, it is hoped that most government officials would not act in an unfair and malicious manner and it is hoped that this case is an aberrant situation simply not recognized by this court.

The court missed the root cause of the malicious actions and behavior of the government officials established at the start of this project. The discovery process allowed us to weigh the actions "behind the scenes" and the actual actions and behavior. The court did not factor in the blatant goal to terminate and destroy the small HubZone business to teach this contractor and others the lesson that they cannot (1) protest and win; and (2) defeat or change the age old practices and relationship with the small niche of big business housing contractors. There is no reason or any other justification of such actions and behavior to destroy a small disadvantaged business. The actions by the government officials were malicious and used to extort and extract benefit to the government's contractual obligations. Their actions are not in accordance with law and the contract.

Two federal judges identified the unfair and improper treatment of the HubZone Contractor. These actions were not addressed then or now and the only impact was the added litigation cost to the contractor. Most importantly the CFC failed to recognize that the government violated the public trust as determined by at least two federal judges. Arbitrary and capricious actions are not an accident, it is intentional. **There is no way the violation of the public trust would allow the presumption of good faith in this contract when it is realized that the Navy's actions were arbitrary and capricious.** It is unfair for the CFC to ignore the findings of the two previous federal judges and to characterize the HUBZone contractor as a "litigation-driven interpreter of the contract."

The principles that the court relied on for this decision did not address malicious and abusive actions and behavior by the government. These principles are described in the court decision. First, government workers are "...**presumed to carry out their duties in good faith**". Second, incompetence on the part of the government officials does not trigger a breach of good faith. "Therefore, incompetence and/or the failure to cooperate or accommodate a contractor's request do not trigger the duty of good faith and fair dealing, unless the Government **"specifically targeted" action to obtain the "benefit of [the] contract" or where Government actions were "undertaken for the purpose of delaying or hampering [performance of the] contract[.]"**

> "Therefore, incompetence and/or the failure to cooperate or accommodate a contractor's request do not trigger the duty of good faith and fair dealing, unless the Government "specifically targeted" action to obtain the "benefit of [the] contract" or where Government actions were "undertaken for the purpose of delaying or hampering [performance of the] contract[.]" Precision Pine, 596 F.3d at 829; see also Malone v. United States, 849 F.2d 1441, 1445-46 (Fed. Cir. 1988) (holding that only where the CO's "evasive conduct misled [plaintiff] to perform roughly 70% of its contractual obligation in reliance on a workmanship standard" was the issue of breach of good faith and fair dealing invoked), pg 15 of the Court of Federal Claims, Civil No. 07-777C.

COURT OF FEDERAL CLAIMS DECISION

3 "Of course a contract may be rendered unenforceable, because of duress, but the plaintiff must establish "(1) that it involuntarily accepted the other party's terms, (2) that circumstances permitted no other alternative, and (3) that such circumstances were the result of the other party's coercive acts." North Star Steel Co. v. United States, 477 F.3d 1324, 1334 (Fed. Cir. 2007) (emphasis added); see also Rumsfeld v. Freedom NY, Inc., 329 F.3d 1320, 1330 (Fed. Cir. 2003) ("'[E]conomic pressure and even the threat of considerable financial loss are not duress.'" (quoting Johnson, Drake & Piper, Inc. v. United States, 531 F.2d 1037, 1042 (Ct. Cl. 1976))). pg 15 of the Court of Federal Claims, Civil No. 07-777C.

Thirdly, in order to prove a breach of the good faith and fair dealings the contractor has to prove that the actions by the government were, "…**specifically designed to reappropriate the benefits of the contract and to abrogate the government's obligations under the contract**". Fourth, a contract may be rendered unenforceable, "…**because of duress, but the plaintiff must establish "(1) that it involuntarily accepted the other party's terms, (2) that circumstances permitted no other alternative, and (3) that such circumstances were the result of the other party's coercive acts."**

In simple lay person logic these principles applied by the CFC means that the government officials can delay the project, or do anything to hinder or hamper the contractor as long as they **don't** or it cannot be proved that their actions or behavior does not result in a benefit to the government. The benefit to the government must abrogate the government's obligations, e.g., reduce the cost or pass the cost to the contractor. Since the government officials are presumed to always act in good faith and if they are incompetent in their jobs or in the performance of their duties they cannot be in breach of the good faith and fair dealing principle of contracting. Simply, an incompetent government official cannot be in bad faith because they are not competent enough to design action(s) to benefit the government. Or they cannot be in breach of the good faith and fair dealing because they are incompetent and cannot cause damage to the government. It appears that the CFC's flawed logic protects the government because the government officials cannot cause damage to the contractor because they are not competent enough to specifically design such actions to benefit the government.

The CFC did not recognize that the assignment of a contracting officer and staff who are not trained, experienced or qualified to administer a $48,000,000.00 design build MILCON project is a gross violation of the public trust. This action alone does not allow reliance on the presumption of good faith because it violates the public's trust for good faith. At the time of the initial assignment the Navy violated the public's trust and breached the duty for good faith and fair dealings.

> For example, the contracting officer who does not know how to read or analyze the schedule, as required by the contract, is incompetent and therefore cannot be expected to negotiate or analyze any effort to extend the time in a contract modification as required by the contract, because they are incompetent. If the contractor is not provided with a fair and equitable time adjustment in the modification to the contract it is because the contracting officer is incompetent and does not have the wherewithal to figure out the benefit to the government.

The court's decision is based on looking at each allegation in the claim individually and applying the above principles. The impact of the actions or behavior that causes damage must be considered in the totality of all the actions to obtain a fair decision. The **total impact** to the project must be considered in the evaluation of bad faith, although not given any consideration in this court's decision. At the end of the day the intent and the consequence of the project must be given due consideration when deciding who and how the impact of each event or decision is considered. The end result of the contract must be a consideration because it reflects the actual conditions and behavior of the project. Above all the CFC failed to recognize the violation of the public's trust that resulted in the failure of the project. At the very least look at what the taxpayer got for the money spent:

Intent of Milcon	End Result
Provide quality residential units for the military and their families to raise the quality of life in a **safe and healthful** environment for the enlisted military.	The project was completed with carcinogen contaminated soils in the front and back yards of the housing units. Unsafe and unhealthful exposures to the families, including the infants and children to a disproportionate risk of cancer. This was done at the expense to the contractor, including delays and liquidated damages.
Congress desires to aid and promote small business through the HubZone program.	This contract puts one small site contractor and the general contractor out of business. The same government officials also ruined another small business in the 8(a) program.

SUMMARY

One cannot help but reach the conclusion that this contractor was treated unfairly from the time they submitted their bid proposal to the end of the contract. The CFC did not recognize the historical facts that reflect the intent to hinder and hamper the contractor. It is disappointing that the CFC decided that the malicious actions and behavior of the government officials is acceptable because of the presumption that they always act in good faith. Their incompetence is acceptable despite the fact that their malicious actions were designed to abrogate the government's obligations. The court decision that the Navy's malicious actions and behavior is not bad faith because they did not abrogate the government's obligations is faulty and is a license to "kill businesses".

A review of the CFC decisions show a failure to evaluate how these actions impacted the project. Each action is synergistic and the impact has to be measured in total and not in a piecemeal fashion. All of the actions and behavior of the government officials are related and had significant impacts to the failure of this project. For example one of the most significant actions is the requirement to use a schedule that the government cannot use, yet it is downplayed by the CFC. The CFC decision about the schedule is reduced to a simple contract requirement. The court rules that the contract specification requires the Primavera SureTrak and therefore the delay and subsequent impact to the project is ignored or downplayed. In this instance the manipulation of the schedule is crucial to many subsequent actions related:

(1) to controlling the project schedule and not allowing the design-build contractor to control his own project;

(2) not recording the delays and the analysis of the time impacts to show delays and the late completion date allows the government officials to hold retention which is later used to bribe and extort benefits from the contractor;

(3) using the retention, which is the monies that the contractor has already earned, to bribe the contractor to performing work or to accepting modifications;

The malicious actions and behavior of the government officials cannot be presumed in good faith if it violates the rules, regulations, and laws. More importantly the violation of the public's trust must be weighed in the overall decision and must remain a primary factor for fairness. The principle that the government officials are presumed to always act in good faith is understood to apply to those who "act in good faith". The public's trust holds that these individuals and agencies operate in a higher standard of performance and ethics because they were given this presumption of good faith. The presumption of good faith is a sacred trust given by the public and must be preserved when it is applied in good faith. When the public's trust is violated the illicit and the destructive actions by the government must be dealt with harshly. The police officer that acts aggressively to save a life is understood to act in good faith and he must be protected. However, the standards of behavior and the level of performance are at levels far higher than the average citizen. The level of performance and the accountability must meet the high level that is trusted by the public.

The assignment of contracting personnel who are not qualified, experienced or educated to administer a contract of this size is the first step in the long string of violations to the public trust which is ignored by the CFC. There is no way that the government can justify disregarding the laws, rules and regulations of the contract and the intentional destruction of the contractor by holding earned monies and restricting cash flow, blackmailing the contractor to accept illicit modifications, and to intentionally delay the contract to build liquidated damages. These are only examples of the complete disregard for their obligations to earn the public trust.

It is disappointing and discouraging to read the CFC decision and recognize that the violation of the public trust will continue. It cannot and should not be tolerated as a defense to allow the types of actions and behavior so blatantly carried out in this contract. We must speak up and protest so this kind of behavior does not continue.

The failure of the government to maintain a high level of performance and to ensure the high level of standards to ensure the public's trust is atrocious. The CFC's responsibility to protect the public's trust and to preserve the presumption of good faith for government officials MUST be based on the integrity of our system. The CFC cannot allow the violation of the contract and law to be ignored and justified by incompetence and the use of the presumption of good faith. Citizens are disappointed and we are concerned that the public's trust is not as sacred as we thought it was. An appeal for the integrity and preservation of the public's trust must be submitted.

> "There may be times when we are powerless to prevent injustice, but there must never be a time when we fail to protest." Elie Wiesel, Romanian born American Writer. Nobel Prize for Peace in 1986.

15

Appellate Court Decision

The decision by the United States Court of Federal Claims (CFC) was issued on December 9, 2011, four years after the claim was filed. The court excused the fraud, waste and abuse of authority by allowing the government officials the assumption of good faith despite the recognition of their gross incompetence. The appellate court did not agree and vacated the CFC decision. Without this understanding of the events and the "narrow view" of the CFC we would have been stuck with a decision that would allow the abuse of authority as described by the CFC.

> *"Short of such interference, it is well established that federal officials are presumed to act in good faith, so that "[a]ny analysis of a question of Governmental bad faith must begin with the presumption that public officials act conscientiously in the discharge of their duties." See Kalvar Corp. v. United States, 543 F.2d 1298, 1301 (Ct. Cl. 1976) (internal quotation marks and citation omitted); see also Spezzaferro v. Fed. Aviation Admin., 807 F.2d 169, 173 (Fed. Cir. 1986) ("Government officials are <u>presumed to carry out their duties in good faith</u>.").*
>
> *Therefore, incompetence and/or the failure to cooperate or accommodate a contractor's request do not trigger the duty of good faith*

APPELLATE COURT DECISION

and fair dealing, <u>unless the Government "specifically targeted" action to obtain the "benefit of [the] contract" or where Government actions were "undertaken for the purpose of delaying or hampering [performance of the] contract[.]"</u>

It appears that the logic of this decision is explained by the incompetence of the government officials. In the court's decision it seems that incompetent contracting officers and personnel cannot be guilty of bad faith because they are incompetent and not smart enough to specifically target actions or undertake the purpose of delaying or hampering the contractor. The long list of malicious actions taken by the government to hinder and hamper the contractor is judged individually by the CFC. The impact of each action was not considered in total. The synergistic consequences of these malicious actions are excused by the CFC using the above logic.

> For example, the delay of the project to require a change in the scheduling software is addressed by the CFC by simply stating that the contract specifications require this software. The fact that none of the government officials were trained or experienced to use this software is ignored. The fact that the government did not comply with any of the contract specifications for the schedule is ignored. Specifically, the contract specifications require time impact analyses to be used for time extensions and yet none of the time extensions issued by the government is based on any time impact analysis using this software. Further the use of the justifiable data from the scheduling software is required to approve payments, yet none of the payments were based on this data.

Each of the allegations discussed in the HUBZone contractor claim involve a long string of consequences that impact on each other. The synergism that is associated with these actions and the consequences should not have been ignored. In totality their actions and the subsequent consequences leads to the establishment of bad faith and unfair dealings.

The HUBZone contractor could not let this illogical decision to remain on the books and to be used in other cases. The Associated General Contractors of America, the Associated Builders and Contractors, Inc., and the Design Build Institute of America submitted Amicus Curiae briefs to the appellate court. As noted in the Associated General Contractors of America Amicus Curiae brief the government is required to act reasonably and if not they are liable:

> *"For many years, the burden required to prove that the government breached its duty of good faith and fair dealing has been equally well settled. The longstanding rule is that a plaintiff need not prove governmental bad faith—which requires clear and convincing evidence of intent. See Abcon Assocs. v. United States, 49 Fed. Cl. 678, 688 (2001); see also Universal Shelters of Am., Inc. v. United States, 87 Fed. Cl. 127, 145 (2009). Indeed, "[i]f plaintiff establishes by a preponderance of evidence that the challenged actions were unreasonable, the Government cannot elude liability...." San Carlos Irrigation and Drainage Dist. v. United States, 84 Fed. Cl. 786, 804 (emphasis added)"*

The preponderance of the evidence provided in the HUBZone contractor claim included a long list of significant actions that were unreasonable. By any measure of common sense these examples are undoubtedly classified as unreasonable actions by the government. Some of the undisputable examples of unreasonable behavior that caused hindering and hampering of the project are:

- Delaying the project to require scheduling software that could not be used by the government.

- Not complying with the contractual requirements regarding the scheduling and the payments.

APPELLATE COURT DECISION

- Not approving the most qualified and experienced managers for the contractor's management team to manipulate the management of the project.

- Disqualifying numerous highly qualified and experienced Quality Control managers to require the contractor to hire the "friend" of the government official. A $240,000.00 contract is awarded to the "friend" of the government official.

- By forcing the manipulation of the schedule to improperly justify the holding of payments, i.e., retention. The retention of monies is used to bribe and coerce the contractor in to signing change orders and to give up valid requests for equitable adjustment.

- Delaying the project for 14 months to "investigate" the differing site conditions related to expansive soils. Not only does this hold up the project but the government secretly plotted to terminate the contractor during this 14 month period.

- Delaying the project for at least 7 months while the government plotted to justify the contamination of the housing projects with known carcinogens.

- The deliberate declaration of "war" against the contractor and deliberate actions to delay inspections and turnover of the completed housing. These delays are intended to drive up the liquidated damages costs against the contractor.

The appeal was filed in the United States Court of Appeals for the Federal Circuit and on February 11, 2014 the court vacated the decision by the CFC and remanded the case back to the CFC. It is a relief that the appellate court recognized the unreasonable behavior of the government officials. The appellate court ruled:

- "We hold that the Court of Federal Claims misread our precedent in articulating what the contractor, _____ Construction Company, needed to show in order to prove that the government breached that duty. We also hold that the trial court misinterpreted certain contractual provisions related to _____ (HUBZone contractor) good-faith-and-fair-dealing claim. We therefore vacate the trial court's decision that _____ (HUBZone contractor) failed to establish liability, vacate the accompanying damages award, and remand for further proceedings using the correct standard."

The rationale and the methodologies applied by the government officials throughout this contract can only be classified as shameful misconduct and incompetence. These officials are not experienced or knowledgeable of the standards, rules, regulations, and the principles of contracting and design build projects. Their conduct does not reflect a high regard for their duties. As a matter of fact their complete disregard for the rules for fraud, waste and abuse of authority is reflected at all levels of the management staff. The lack of accountability and the continued support to disregard their duty is the root cause of this atrocity.

At the end of the day the appellate court vacates the CFC decision and remands the case back to be re-evaluated. As we live through this total destruction of the contractor's business and personal lives from 2002 to 2014 to find that we are back to square one with the CFC can be somewhat frustrating. This contractor was the victim of abuse of authority at least since 2002 when the contract bid for this project was first submitted and thrown out illegally. Twelve years fighting to build quality and safe housing for military families is thwarted at the end by the deliberate contamination of the topsoil throughout the project. Today we learn that hundreds of military families have been suffering and mistreated because of the contaminated housing project. Their complaints are ignored as they suffer with unexplained illnesses.

The methods used by the government contracting staff for this

APPELLATE COURT DECISION

project continued to act in violation of the assumption of good faith. They publicized and boasted of their win after the December 2011 CFC decision. The destruction and crippling of small businesses and the abuse of authority are considered their outstanding accomplishments. Their actions are a complete waste of the taxpayer's monies and the violation of the trust given to them. After 12 years the project costs were shamefully wasted and the housing is sitting on carcinogen contaminated lands. No one will be held accountable and the victims of the abuse and negligence are the contractor, subcontractors and financial institutions that supported the contractor. Most importantly no one will be held accountable for the complete disregard for the health of the military families who have been paying for the lack of regard for their safety.

We found that the Navy's administration of this contract was a horrific and blatant disregard for their duty to act in good faith. More importantly we discover that the Navy officials will direct the actions to mislead the public and the military families. The process to direct the human health risk assessment does not come close to an adequate assessment of exposures to human life. The arrogant attitude that the exposure will only be for "6 years" and the manipulation of exposure levels is safe is not fully supported. The Navy simply makes a declaration that it is safe and they proceed to expose the unsuspecting military families and children.

The Navy is well aware of the significant health effects regarding the use and placement of these carcinogenic pesticides for many many years. The Office of Naval Research issued a contract for the study of pesticides to control termites PRIOR to the 1988 EPA ban of most of these pesticides. The health assessment dealt with the exposures in military family housing. The health assessment was conducted by the National Research Council (US) Committee on Toxicology and their report was issued in 1982. Their report, *"An Assessment of the Health Risks of Seven Pesticides Used for Termite Control"*, specifically address their concerns with the exposure to military families and these pesticides. The Navy knew or should have known of their own research that would not have allowed the construction of homes on carcinogen contaminated land for our military families.

The Navy becomes a partner with a private venture and they both continue the practice of constructing homes for the military families on carcinogen contaminated lands. Military parents are inundated with unexplained illnesses after they move in to the base housing residences. Their pets are sick and many of them die of convulsions, tumors, cancer, and other undetermined causes. The unexplained illnesses continue to affect their children, pets and themselves. In 2013 they learn of the contamination and they are furious. Military families are not informed of the contaminated lands and the low level exposures. The medical community is also not informed of the contaminated lands and it presents a serious obstacle in the healthcare providers' ability to direct the proper testing and diagnosis of ailments. A lawsuit is filed. There was no reason for constructing homes for our military families on carcinogen contaminated lands. THIS IS TRULY THE CONTRACT FROM HELL.

CPSIA information can be obtained at www.ICGtesting.com
Printed in the USA
BVOW11s1737180914

367384BV00004B/12/P